# JOURNEYS

Finding Life's Way in Spite of Obstacles

Alison Ridley Evans                    Dr. Carl W. Mores

Curtis F. Garfield

Porcupine Enterprises
Sudbury, Massachusetts 01776

*"A disability does not necessarily affect accomplishments in any field, however, talent does."*

Itzhak Perlman

I

ABOUT THE AUTHORS

Alison Ridley Evans has written (with Curt Garfield) *The Story of the Lygon Arms* (one of the world's most famous hostelries in Worcestershire, England), *As Ancient Is This Hostelry* (The Story of the Wayside Inn of Sudbury, Massachusetts) and most recently *Henry Ford's Boys*.

Dr. Carl W. Mores has spent much of his life working with children with disabilities. He has been an educator at all levels, a public and independent school Head, and public speaker for some thirty years. He was recently selected as Executive of the Year by the National Association of Private Schools for Exceptional Children.

Curt Garfield has worked as a newspaper columnist, Senior Editor of *New England Out of Doors Magazine* and Associate Editor of *Saltwater Sportsman*. He is a winner of eight first places in New England Outdoor Writer's Association contests. Together with Alison Evans he has written *As Ancient Is This Hostelry, Henry Ford's Boys,* and *The Story of Lygon Arms* and is the co-author of *Power Surfcasting* with Ron Arra.

# ACKNOWLEDGMENTS

Subsequently in the course of creating this book, a great many people have helped in ways both direct and indirect. We try below to acknowledge them.

The idea for this book originated with Carl Mores, Executive Director/President of Cotting School in Lexington, Massachusetts, to whom must go the credit for the original inspiration and impetus for the whole endeavor. Several years ago he had an idea which gradually grew into reality. This reality is, in large measure, due to his unwavering persistence.

We extend our gratitude to all the subjects of the chapters, who graciously volunteered their time to tell us their life stories and to correct the chapters in progress. Each of them has individual ability in his or her chosen field and all of them together have the wisdom and patience to recognize the importance of sharing these stories with others.

A number of individuals were instrumental in helping us to establish contact with the subjects in the chapters and to follow and maintain these contacts over the months of interviews and exchange of letters. We should like to mention, in particular, Michele Konishi, Press Secretary to Senator Daniel K. Inouye of Hawaii, Paul Cantor and Donald Marse, agents for Diane Schuur, and Tina Stringer, assistant to Darryl Stingley in the Darryl Stingley Youth Foundation. They were all courteous, prompt and provided indispensable and ongoing assistance. Our warmest thanks to all of them.

We are grateful to the Association of Mouth and Foot Painting Artists who supplied us with the name of Nancy Litteral, Chapter 7.

Barbara Hardaway, Chapter 4, injected the whole enterprise with her own brand of humor and and joie de vivre. She advised us at several points and helped us to continue despite setbacks. Her talents as a vibrant, vital human being are as outstanding as her abilities as a multifaceted artist, teacher and writer.

We should like to acknowledge the continuing help of Patricia Dabrowney, Executive Secretary to Dr. Mores, who has had to deal, over nearly three years, with a barrage of telephone calls, inquiries, strange requests and deadlines. She has met all these with courteous efficiency and has been an important member of the team.

Lastly, Alison Evans and Curtis Garfield would like to extend their warmest thanks to Richard Aparo, Chapter 1, a friend and colleague for many years. He has collaborated with us in a number of literary and historical ventures and in political campaigns. He, more than anyone else, taught us the language and mores of "the challenged," until we gradually felt at ease talking with these travelers and gained confidence to do so. Without Rick's patient counsel, this book would not have come into being.

# *DEDICATION*

The authors proudly dedicate this work

to those many persons whose journeys have,

in spite of obstacles, demonstrated much

courage and accomplishment.

# Introduction

Today was particularly difficult. On such days I often walk the corridors and visit the classrooms of the great school where I work. On this day I met a child in her wheelchair, sitting alone in a quiet spot, gently sobbing. I knelt by her chair to offer comfort. She said, "it was all so hard today. Nothing worked and I tried so hard." I honestly responded, "me, too! Today has been a really tough one for me. That's why I came to see you."

The little girl looked at me directly and said, "Really? I thought that you were always in charge. I didn't know that you had hard days like I do. Usually when I'm upset people don't want to talk with me. You don't seem to be like that......," her voice trailed away.

We sat quietly for a few minutes. There was no magic, no sudden healings. But a young child who felt all alone and discouraged and an aging man who was overwhelmed by the cares of a hard day, shared a moment of humanness, unusual understanding, even encouragement. As we parted she said, "Thank-you for being my friend. I'll be o.k. now."

I see this child occasionally as she manages her wheelchair quite successfully but with difficulty. We catch each other's eyes and a exchange a special little wave. We both know that we helped each other even though a great chasm of years separated us.

We routinely stoop to enter cars and airplanes, to plug a cord into an electric outlet, to reach under a chair. Unless I was willing to stoop to talk to a child, I could not have looked into her sad eyes or gained entry into her heart. In bending down and reaching out, both of us were encouraged.

In the pages of this book there are stories of encouragement. Each story contains examples of great challenge but each one includes real examples of "overcoming the odds." In these stories, find words of hope.

Although Jean Driscoll won the Boston Marathon seven times, she regards her second place finish in 1997, as her greatest triumph. "We are not just the courageous disabled," she says, "we make mistakes, have accidents, have to get up and go on, like everyone else...." That is what she did in 1997 after her hard fall and that is what she has done over and over again throughout her life. Her life is an inspiration. Her transition from being a discouraged child to an international wheelchair athlete has not been easy. It required courage and determination. She and the others described in this book, are examples to all of us to be all we can be, to help one another, where and when we can, and whenever possible to provide opportunities for others to help themselves to be all that they can be. In doing so each of us is strengthened.

A few people seem to know naturally that their actions will be controlled by their current obsessions and desires. They have an ability for optimism that others cannot seem to develop.

When the window narrows...When a depressed person speaks of hopelessness, she may say that there is no future. Every possibility of any meaningful future seems to be utterly cut off.

When a merely anxious or worried person speaks of hopelessness, he means that the future is dark but a window of hope remains. All is not lost. He may need to focus on clearer, realizable goals in order to build step-by-step confidence for bigger challenges ahead. Sometimes we must focus on the small light that still penetrates the dark times in order to gather ourselves for another day.

A friend can no longer speak. He cannot care for himself. Gradually, the awful darkness of ALS has grasped his body ever more tightly. Yet it has been said of him, "This is a man of strength, climbing mountains." And he has said, "one has to decide whether to stay fighting or simply cave in."

Many of us cannot relate to such determination in the face of terrible debilitating disease. But each of us certainly can be encouraged and challenged to renew our own hope in the midst of difficult times. And when hope includes truly caring for others, we are enlarged as persons. We grow more generous. Our spirits rise.

Barbara Hardaway contracted polio at age three and has since lived in braces or in a wheelchair. She rejoices in her "Beautiful Braces" series — collages of bits and pieces of former leg braces she has saved over the years which she can now celebrate as important and even beautiful in her life. She speaks of her spiritual journey and encourages each of us to rediscover and challenge the "braces" in our lives so that we, too, can celebrate our own beauty.

Everyone has something about which there seems to be no beauty. In our time there are so many young people who for some reason or other do not think of themselves as at all attractive. The commercials would have us believe that beauty is to be found in products or in a perfectly shaped body.

Having struggled mightily, Dr. Hardaway has found beauty within and it pushes to the outside as well. She is extraordinarily attractive, but she is truly a beautiful person because her perspective on life is an exciting daily example for her students and others. "You, too, can celebrate your beauty," she would tell us.

Within the pages that follow, you will meet twelve wonderful people who will inspire you to do this. This book was written to introduce you to each of them and through meeting them, to be encouraged and challenged.

Carl Mores

# Table of Contents

## A GLASS HALF FULL

**Richard Aparo, Senior Engineer at ADE Corporation**

Richard Aparo,
Senior Engineer at ADE Corporation

# A GLASS HALF FULL

## Richard Aparo, Senior Engineer at ADE Corporation

"The biggest benefit of being handicapped is that it improves the quality of the people around you," Richard (Rick) Aparo remarked cheerfully in June 1996. Rick Aparo is an exceptionally talented engineer who works in the development engineering department of ADE Corporation. "When I was a child, I was afflicted with 'cuteness' and attracted all sorts of people. When you are in a wheelchair the phonies fade away rather quickly. I am blessed by being surrounded almost exclusively by genuine human beings."

Aparo, who fell from a dormitory window when he was a sophomore at M.I.T., and broke a vertebra in his back, runs his life on metal forearm crutches or from a wheelchair. He is now 50 years old, married, with an 11-year-old son.

His injury was the result of some weekend hijinks at the dorm. Having been barricaded into his room by some mirthful compatriots, he, with the determined sense of humor and competitiveness which has characterized his life before and since, made a rope of sheets and attempted escape through a third-floor window. "I failed to properly engineer the rope, which was too short to reach the ledge I was aiming for. I had to jump about 25 feet to the ground. I broke only one bone, but sadly it was not the best choice of bone to be broken.."

After spending five months at Massachusetts General Hospital, three months in bed healing a spinal-fusion that was performed only a few hours after the injury, followed by two months of rehabilitation, he returned to M.I.T to finish earning his degree. He graduated with a Bachelor of Science degree in 1971. He had initially concentrated on math and physics, "with a brief flirtation with biology," but ended up majoring in computer science.

"This was a good place to be in those days if you wanted to be employed after college." Rick's greatest problem at M.I.T., after the injury was sheer lack of mobility. "M.I.T. is difficult for anyone to handle. My dorm was three blocks from the classrooms, so I spent a lot of time just getting from place to place. I had a car with hand-controls, but parking is such a problem there that it was really little help. My classmates were helpful and sympathetic in getting me through."

When he graduated, Rick went home for a short time to Chicago. His grandparents had all been immigrants from various parts of Italy and Germany and he had strong family ties in the mid-West, but soon realized that he was not going to get the right kind of job there. "The centers for the business I was interested in were in San Francisco, Texas, and Boston, so I came back to Boston, where I had friends who could take me in while I got started. I 'crashed' with old school chums in their dorms and apartments while I looked for work."

It was 1971 and the engineering profession was in a depression. After a couple of fruitless months, he went to the Massachusetts Division of Employment Security to apply for assistance, be it welfare or work. They found him a contract job with their first phone-call "as a technical-writer for a small company (now extinct) called Black and White Enterprises. I finally could afford to pay a share of the rent."

After a short career as a technical writer, Rick found an engineering job at a start-up company called Ross Controls in 1972, which was bought out of bankruptcy by another small company, Memodyne, in 1975. He moved on to the medical division of Hewlett-Packard in 1981, which in 1986 granted him a one-year fellowship to obtain a master's degree in software engineering from the Wang Institute (now defunct). Shortly after his job was relocated from Waltham, Mass. to more distant Andover, Mass., he left HP to join ADE Corporation in November 1995.

Asked about difficulties he encountered in adjusting to working in the world of computers, Rick claims they were minimal. "I was doing what I was trained to do and my hampered mobility was no impediment to doing it well. I never contemplated a career such as competing in sports where my injury could have been a barrier, so becoming handicapped was not a big

5

loss to me."

Rick, who is fit and trim, exercises regularly at candlepin bowling. He delivers the ball standing, supported by a single crutch, and walks back and forth to keep the score, putting himself through an exacting workout. He typically scores in the high nineties and low hundreds.

The two accomplishments in business of which Rick is proudest are, first, his completion and introduction of a microprocessor based digital cassette recorder while he was at Memodyne. This project required electronics, software, and mechanical design, almost all of which he did himself. "That project really launched me as an engineer. I learned so much doing it and found my niche: interdisciplinary engineering."

His second major achievement came at Hewlett-Packard where he integrated ten cards worth of microprocessor and memory circuits into a single card of the same size. "This was another multidiscipline project that I designed pretty much on my own, but the real challenge was getting past all the nay-sayers." This circuit card went into production in 1993 and started saving HP 3.6 million dollars per year. "We were short on new products that year, so marketing printed up fliers trumpeting the improvement in reliability my new card made possible."

Despite his successes at Hewlett-Packard, over the long-term Rick did not enjoy working for this large organization. "It is rather a political place." he says. "You can't get ahead just by doing good work; you have to 'play ball' with people who cannot understand what you are doing and are often suspicious and obstructionist.

"You might think it hard to leave after 14 years, but in fact it was very easy for me." At dinner with an old friend from high school and college days who worked for ADE Corporation, Rick learned that they were expanding and actually offering a bounty for engineers with his skills. Within a few weeks Rick was at his current position.

Rick's wife, Helen, who is a doctor at Beth Israel Hospital, has been and remains a major force in his life. He explains, with humor, that although he dated starting in college "doing things that did not involve dancing" he took his time getting married. "I joined a video-dating service. One went in and answered six questions in front of a camera and then people came in and viewed each others tapes and selected whom they wished to meet. Before I joined, the saleswoman and I had a long talk, first about whether their service was appropriate for me, then about whether and how I should reveal my handicap. Despite my 'on-air confession', I had wonderful response to my tape and had numerous dates with lovely women and finally found Helen."

Helen and Rick met for the first time shortly before Halloween in 1985. Their first contact was a Sunday phone call in which they discovered that they were both so busy that there was no day in the near future when they could meet, so they met a few hours later at the Wok in Wellesley. Their courtship proceeded at a rapid pace after that and they married in April 1987.

After their son, Christopher, was born, both Rick and Helen had to do some tough juggling of schedules. "When Helen was 'attending physician' at the hospital, we could just about write her off for the month," he recalls. "Whenever she wasn't working, I was. The three of us were seldom together for very long. Also, we have a very bright, active son, hard for the ordinary day care person to keep up with.

"It was both difficult and expensive in the beginning, not quite so much now with Christopher in school. In the early days, I occasionally had to take an entire day off from work, especially if Christopher was sick." 'Active' and 'difficult' or not, it is clear that Rick and Helen are very proud of their intelligent child.

Rick's interests are not limited to his professional activities. He has been interested in politics for a long time and was a participant in several campaigns. He is an independent, choosing candidates, not parties, and is proud of this fact. With his keen mind and organizational ability, he is invaluable in the helter-skelter pressures of a campaign.

In 1980, he worked in the presidential campaign of John B. Anderson, first as a Republican in the primaries, and then as an Independent when the candidate mounted a third-party effort. Rick stood as an elector, allowing his name and address to be printed on all the petition sheets used to get the candidate on the Massachusetts ballot. He worked as a coordinator for the 10th congressional district (which racked-up the highest percentage of votes in the Commonwealth).

Since then Rick has served as a precinct captain for Congressman Barney Frank and worked in the Gary Hart campaign for president. Asked if he has considered running for office himself, Rick responded cautiously: "I would only do it if I was pushed into it, simply because there are so many people out there desperately seeking office and willing to sacrifice everything, including honor, to make their mark. I would never want to be someone like that."

He maintained that although to him politics and public life are not distasteful, it is growing harder and harder to find suitable people who are willing to run because any mistake they may have made in their life is dragged up and magnified in the glare of publicity. "No one has a perfect life, and if they did, they would not have sufficient experience to function effectively in public office."

Rick's view of society's attitude toward the handicapped is somewhat unusual. "The problem is not wheelchair ramps, which are easily built, but human nature, which is hard to change. Any form of diversity seems frightening to many people. They cannot accept someone who is different in any respect. People with annoying laughs can have as much of a problem socially as someone in a wheelchair.

"If people were more open-minded, no matter how great the differences, they might find they could incorporate the unusual in their perception of normal. After all, everyone is different in some way and there are so many spheres in which we can succeed or fail in other peoples' eyes.

Just by saying you like a particular candidate or that you are pro-choice or pro-life can hurtle you into an unfortunate category in someone's estimation. Being unable to walk is just another in a vast array of problems one must deal with in everyday life."

Rick feels that technology, and computers specifically, have helped handicapped people by creating a lot more sedentary jobs. "This is a good thing if you are immobile. It has created, for the first time, a whole new class of job, jobs which are remote. You can be a software engineer from your home–from your bed for that matter.

"This has happened dramatically during the last decade. We are not talking about 'make work' but about really needed and useful jobs. They require trained judgment and well developed communication skills."

His advice to the newly physically challenged: "Step one is to think about what you have, what are the resources that still exist, and be careful in writing things off, in determining that you don't have certain capabilities. Take inventory of what you have and make the most of every bit of that instead of dwelling on what you can't do. If you can't stop focusing on the things that are gone, you are headed for a life that will not be worth anything."

Rick also has advice for the friends and relatives of those who have become handicapped, drawn from his own experience. He observes that just about everyone he has made friends with since his injury has "gone through a visible process of mourning. I see the signs: denial, expectations of my imminent recovery, a miracle. The trouble with this is that my handicap often becomes invisible to the point where they expect me to do things that are impossible. My little son has urged me to just get up and walk, certain that if only I tried I could do it.

"Adults have expected that I could walk down the street eating an ice-cream cone, but when you have both hands occupied by crutches you can't carry anything that insists on being held right-side-up." Even his beloved wife is not immune: "sometimes allowing the furniture to get in the way of wheelchair access." He emphasizes that exactly the wrong thing to do is to take the attitude that the handicapped person does not need this or that access because someone else is going to take care of things for him.

"Someone like myself wants to do things for himself. It takes longer, but people just have to be patient. I enjoy cooking and do it often; I recently cooked a vat of chili for the ADE Chili Fest. However, I have to be able to get into the kitchen in my wheelchair to do it."

Rick cited other problems he encounters. He has always enjoyed traveling and has been to Europe several times since his injury. "You have to be clever about packing and how you will be able to carry stuff. I use backpacks and duffel bags that I can carry on my back while walking on my crutches. I find cardboard boxes that fit well into my duffel bag to stiffen it to protect my clothes. Showers are a problem too. In an inexpensive room, especially abroad, you will find a shower, not a tub. If you can't stand up, that is a big problem.

In his business life, Rick has been faced with the dilemma of the "Uppity Cripple." (He admits borrowing the phrase from Supreme Court Justice Clarence Thomas, who referred to himself as an "uppity black.") A macho man confronted with a woman who may be more capable of doing some task than himself may be resentful. When an able-bodied man is confronted with a more capable man on crutches, the result is often the same. It is difficult to get some people to cooperate when you need to be the one calling the shots. People do not react well when they perceive that they are shown up by someone they regard as intrinsically inferior.

Rick advises those who have any kind of handicap to "get beyond the commonplace limitations. Some people will react negatively to your unorthodox efforts to function independently. You have to be creative enough to find ways that you can function and then you have to allow yourself to do things in awkward, socially embarrassing ways. For example, I find in the office that crutches are far less threatening to people than my wheelchair, but I have to use my wheelchair to carry things-books for instance-even if it is only three doors away and even if it is unsettling to others."

An hour or two spent talking with Rick Aparo is educational and inspiring. His mind is so quick and his manner so charming that it does not take long for the handicap to become semi-invisible as he points out. One is dominated by his mind and his evident skills. Anyone who has worked in a political campaign with him over several months is impressed with his lightning perceptions, his ability to deal skillfully with all kinds and conditions of people, his good judgement in a crisis, his avoidance of confrontations, and his unfailing good humor.

He makes a final point: "There is one nugget, one old chestnut I'd like to mention. If you are disabled, handicapped or impaired in any way, think of a glass half full, not a glass half empty. Look at what's still in the glass, not what's missing from it. It's still a GLASS HALF FULL. And so is your life."

# DO THE MOST WITH WHAT YOU HAVE

## Dave Clark

Dave Clark
Courage is the Name of His Game

# DO THE MOST WITH WHAT YOU HAVE

## Dave Clark

Dave Clark has crowded a lifetime's worth of athletic accomplishments into his first 45 years and done so despite contracting polio before his first birthday. But his proudest accomplishment has nothing to do with sport.

"I've played pro baseball, and ice hockey to the collegiate club level," he said in the summer of 1997. "I've coached baseball and scouted for major league teams. I've broadcast sports on the radio. I was involved with the '96 Olympic Games in Atlanta, and I've met President and Mrs. Clinton at the White House. But the accomplishment I'm proudest of is my relationship with my parents and brothers. We are all best friends. It's a unique relationship."

Some trying times have forged that relationship. Ten months after he was born in Corning, New York in 1952, Dave Clark's parents, Bernard and Lillian Clark, were told that their son had contracted a severe case of polio and probably would not live. While he did survive, he had to face a childhood of leg braces and crutches. His parents decided early on not to send him to a "special" school where mobility would have been easier, but to "mainstream" him in a public school system where he quickly discovered that participation in sports was the key to being accepted by his fellow students.

"Had my parents made the decision to send me to a special school, I might never have become an athlete," he said. "By being mainstreamed, I was forced to interact with so-called 'normal' kids AND to try and compete with them in all kinds of activities. That alone was a big challenge.

"Sports came naturally to me even as a youngster and I found it was my way out of the stereotype of being disabled. The better I performed as an athlete, the more my peers accepted me."

In school, Clark played first base and outfield. To the consternation of his parents, he discovered that if he simply took off one of his braces-- against doctor's orders--it gave him more mobility and speed. He has played baseball that way ever since.

His school days had their difficulties. "The attitudes of my fellow students varied," he said. "Some were overly helpful, which I hated but didn't have the heart to tell them. Others treated me like any other kid and still others were downright mean. I still remember one kid in particular who used to call me 'Oleo" meaning 'Polio.' I hated that with a passion and got even by beating him up in a fight later in that school year. I was called into the principal's office and punished for this incident, but the personal satisfaction was well worth it."

Clark's competitiveness at school and his gradual acceptance by other youngsters influenced his later life. Because he was not given preferential treatment at home, his ups and downs were those of any kid growing up and not tied to his disability. "Parents should always try to make their disabled child feel as valuable and as good as anybody else," he explained. "This allows the child to grow up with less insecurity. My parents and brothers, Dan and Doug, are a big part of my success story because they allowed me to try anything I wanted. They weren't overprotective."

Clark joined Little League as soon as he was eligible and got a boost from two understanding coaches, Phil Ritz, and his dad Bernard Clark. Teachers Marjorie Wheeler and Joseph Corcoran also instilled confidence. "They made me feel I could achieve anything I wanted if I put my mind to it and worked hard," he said.

Working hard got him into Corning Community College and then Ithaca State, after which he pursued graduate studies at Ohio State University. During the summers, from 1971 to 1981, he pitched for minor league and semipro baseball teams. He was player-manager and later, owner of the Indianapolis Clowns, a barnstorming baseball team that once helped Hank Aaron break into professional baseball.

In addition, he was head coach at Corning Community College for six years and started Ocala Pro Baseball Camp at Ocala, Florida for kids eight years old and up. He has carried on his interest in hockey (he was goalkeeper for his college club team) by broadcasting Elmira College games each winter.

Dave Clark's long relationship with Sweden began in 1981 when he was first invited to play with the Rattvik Bets. He injured an elbow that season--the beginning of the end of his playing career. Post-polio syndrome set in during the 1987 baseball campaign and he had to retire as a player in 1988, but that didn't stop his baseball career.

In the early 1990s, he was invited back to Sweden as manager of the Rattvik Bets. In 1995 he moved on to the Leksand Lumberjacks, as pitching coach. Leksand is in the same Swedish Elite League as Rattvik. Dave served in the same capacity in 1996 and became the club's manager for the 1997 season. He also became coach of the Swedish National Junior Team.

In Falun, Sweden, Dave met Camilla Ahnstrom, who became his wife in 1995. Sweden has become a second home for Dave Clark; he and his wife spend about half of every year in her country.

Clark's remarkable sports career includes serving as Information Director for the U.S. Olympic baseball tournament at Atlanta in 1996 and scouting for the Baltimore Orioles, New York Yankees, Chicago White Sox, Florida Marlins, and Atlanta Braves. In April 1996, he was one of six recipients of the Giant Steps Award for coaching, sponsored by Northeastern University and presented by President Clinton at the White

House.

"He's a very likeable guy," said Clark of the President. "The impression I got was that he'd love to have the time just to sit down and talk about sports for a while."

Clark finds that conditions for physically challenged people are not as good in Sweden and other parts of Europe as they are in America. "There is no mandate. No law requiring access. No ADA," he points out. "Many places cannot be negotiated by a wheelchair, or by a person on crutches. In the winter, ice and snow are not shoveled or salted, so anyone who cannot walk becomes an automatic shut-in."

Sweden, his second home, has other disadvantages. Gasoline costs $6 a gallon and he soon may find himself paying high Swedish taxes because he spends so much time there. His jet-setting lifestyle--two trips at least each year--is fatiguing as well as exciting. In 1997, for instance, he accompanied the Swedish Junior National Team to Hull, England, and the Lumberjacks to Amsterdam in Holland for the Super Cup of Europe.

"Give yourself time to grieve over your 'loss' of function and then just be strong mentally," he tells the newly disabled. "Realize what your limitations are, what your strengths are, and then work on your strengths. Be realistic about what you can and cannot do.

"And don't be afraid to dream. Work hard and always be thinking about ways your dreams can become reality, given the strength you do still possess. Don't feel sorry for yourself or expect others to do so. Dream realistic dreams given your individual situation. Don't expect dreams to come true without a lot of hard work and effort and be prepared to face rejection and failure.

"We all face this at some point in our lives. Pick up the pieces and find another way to get to your goal. Goal setting is very important. Set small, incremental, reachable goals to build confidence and a strong foundation.

"I always point to my own career and say: 'Look what I did with what I have," Clark concludes. "Probably the crux of it will be making sure you're prepared. There's no such thing as luck, it's preparation meeting opportunity."

Back in the '70s when Clark was keeping goal for his high school hockey team, a sportswriter once wrote that: "Courage is the name of his game." That credo has never changed and never will.

## "DREAM BIG AND WORK HARD"

**Jean Driscoll, Seven-Time Boston Marathon Women's Wheelchair Winner**

Jean
She Loves Turning Light Bulbs On!

## "DREAM BIG AND WORK HARD"

### Jean Driscoll, Seven-Time Boston Marathon Women's Wheelchair Winner

Jean Driscoll had been down Heartbreak Hill seven times before. Each time she was leading the wheelchair division of the Boston Marathon. Each time she had won. Once, in 1994, she covered the 26 miles, 385 yards in 1 hour 34 minutes and 22 seconds, a world record which still stands.

The hill was like an old friend. Its summit marked the 21-mile mark--only five miles to the finish in Copley Square--but there were hazards that she knew only too well. The trolley tracks crossed the course at an angle at Cleveland Circle. Catch a wheel in one of them and you could be out of the race in an instant, if not badly injured.

As her racing chair picked up speed going down the hill, Driscoll surveyed the situation behind and ahead and made her plans. Louise Sauvage of Australia was rapidly closing the gap between them and moving up fast from behind. Louise Sauvage who had bested Driscoll by a second in the wheelchair division of the 1997 Los Angeles Marathon in 2:01.00. The same Sauvage who had finished two minutes behind Driscoll at Boston the year before.

Driscoll leaned forward in her chair to decrease wind resistance and pushed to increase her speed. She knew she had to risk moving more aggressively than she customarily did at this point in the course. As she turned sharply to the left to try to pull ahead of Sauvage, one of Driscoll's wheels caught in the trolley tracks and she crashed to the pavement in Cleveland Circle.

Valuable minutes were lost while some police officers and volunteers attempted in vain to inflate a flat tire. Waving them off, she gave chase to Sauvage who had by then taken a sizeable lead. Although her hopes of breaking Clarence DeMar's record of seven Boston victories had evaporated, she finished a triumphant second.

"My crash at Boston was a good thing," she would say later. "It educated participants and spectators around the world. We're not just the courageous disabled who get out there and struggle along--there is strength, athleticism and risk involved--we have accidents and have to get up and go on, like everyone else in racing."

Jean Driscoll thinks and talks like the champion she is. Her philosophy has always been: "if you fall off the horse, get right back up and go on."

Driscoll got into wheelchair racing accidentally. She was recruited to the University of Illinois at age 20 to play on the women's wheelchair basketball team. The summer before moving to Champaign, Illinois, she qualified for the U.S.A. Developmental Track Team. Then she competed in an international track meet in Great Britain in 1987, and was very successful at the meet (in Ailesbury). Basketball and racing went hand in hand for a while at the University of Illinois, and then racing, particularly marathoning, took over.

Life has not always been easy or triumphant. Driscoll was born with spina bifida and grew up with four brothers and sisters and parents James and Angela in Milwaukee, Wisconsin. She attended a regular grade school.

"I was the only kid in my grade school with a disability and the others made fun of my awkward walking style. I had poor self-esteem. I was a target for teasing," she recalls. She longed to participate in sports, but was relegated to keeping score and helping to manage the teams. "I never had the chance to get in there and get dirty."

Worse was to follow. At age 14, she was riding a 10-speed bike, turned a corner fast, and crashed, dislocating one of her hips. Five operations followed; she was in and out of hospitals in a full body cast for the better part of a year, missing most of her freshman and the first semester of her sophomore year in high school. Then she was told the operations had not taken and she would have to get used to crutches and a wheelchair. "I was mad at God for a long time--most of my teens I was very depressed and reactive," she said.

One outlet in a difficult time of growing up was music. The whole family is musical. Jean and her sister sang in the church choir, one brother played the drums, two others the guitar. Jean herself has such a good voice she now sings the national anthem at large outdoor sports events. She composes some of her own music, "Music is my getaway--I play when I'm especially happy or especially sad. It's good for me." She plays and sings at University of Illinois functions and once sang the national anthem at the opening day of the Milwaukee Brewers season.

"One of my goals when I left Milwaukee and went to the University of Illinois was to get a degree," she said. " She earned both a B.A. in Speech and Communications with honors, and an M.S. in Rehabilitation Administration. "Now I can be a well-spoken boss!"

She now does a great deal of "motivational speaking" to students of all ages, church groups, service groups and corporations. "I love turning light bulbs on." She is a national spokesperson for Ocean Spray Cranberries Inc.

Most of her time is spent training and preparing for racing events world-wide. There are only one or two months of the year when she is not actively in training. Jean won a silver medal at the 1992 Summer Olympic Games in Barcelona, Spain, and another in Atlanta in 1996, both 800-meter wheelchair exhibition events. She won four medals in the Paralympic Games in Korea in 1988, and was champion of the women's wheelchair division of the Los Angeles Marathon in 1995 and 1996. She is a four-time varsity letter winner in Wheelchair Basketball and Wheelchair Track at the

University of Illinois.

Jean Driscoll's tenacity, personality and individual style have not only won her fans all over the world, but national media attention on <u>Good Morning America</u>, <u>ABC Nightline</u> and the <u>Today Show</u>. A PBS documentary about her life, "Against the Wind," was aired on 400 public television stations in 1996.

She credits ADA with having educated much of the public for the first time to the fact that "people in my position want to be independent, not dependent. We don't want people to feel as if they need to rush ahead and open doors for us. Some people do need help, but there is still a lot of educating to be done."

Jean Driscoll is an inspiration to many, but her own transition from disabled child to international athlete has been difficult and has required much commitment and determination. When she was young she was told she would always be dependent on her parents. Now she notes with pride: "I've been around the world without them."

World stops include Paris and Japan as well as Korea, Spain, New Zealand and Great Britain. When she was young she was also enjoined: "The best you can hope for is a sit-down job, such as a secretary, working with your hands." She points out with piercing humor: "So I have a sit-down job and I certainly use my hands a lot, but it's not a secretarial job!

"People who have lost the use of their legs and become secretaries do commendable work; I just didn't want to let the predictions of others come true."

Jean delights in admitting that she has invariably had a "prove you wrong" attitude to life. When she was informed she could not walk; she proceeded to walk--with great effort. All it takes, even now, for her to tackle and accomplish a goal is for someone to insist that it is impossible.

Her advice to the newly disabled or those with permanent disabilities: "Dream big and work hard. The only limitations are those you put on yourself or allow others to place on you. It has taken me a long time to learn. I was in despair as a teenager. It's risky to think big, and you must be ready to make sacrifices, ready for setbacks. Get right back on the horse every time you fall off and carry on. But that's the way to be successful at whatever you choose to do."

Jean Driscoll has come to grips with her limitations and gone beyond them. "I view my disability as a characteristic like height or hair color. You can wear platform shoes if you are short or dye your hair. But the characteristics are still there. I get up in the morning, get in my wheelchair and don't think about it the rest of the day, like someone who wears contact lenses or eyeglasses. I take it for granted and get on with my life."

It is a crowded and satisfying life. In the spring of '97, one week's schedule included a 25-kilometer race in Grand Rapids, Michigan; the keynote address at a New England Fellowship of Christian Athletes banquet; and receiving an honorary degree in Humane Letters from the

University of Rhode Island.

Of all her accomplishments, the one that sticks out in her mind is her second place finish at Boston in 1997. "It added a whole different dimension--a sense of drama. I received more press coverage for this world-wide than any of my seven wins in Boston."

# BEAUTIFUL BRACES: A CELEBRATION OF CREATIVITY

Barbara Hardaway

Dr. Barbara Hardaway
Professor, Artist, Motivator

# BEAUTIFUL BRACES: A CELEBRATION OF CREATIVITY

Barbara Hardaway

Barbara Hardaway summarizes her life as "a journey through literature and the performing arts to reach the point where I can create something to put on the wall. I have worked to be able to make collages--this is my 'now space,' which I celebrate. It has all come together. My life went this way in a passion to express myself."

Dr. Hardaway, who has several careers behind her and at least three ongoing at the present, is a vibrant, enthusiastic person. She is proudest of her work as a visual artist. She contracted polio at age three and has lived since on braces or in a wheelchair. One of her chief accomplishments is the "Beautiful Braces" series, which evolved out of "a personal need to celebrate femininity within the context of living with a physical impairment. As a child, the leg braces that I wore were functional, enabling me to learn the art of walking, skipping, and dancing. However, they were also unattractive, not the least bit delicate or pleasing to my eyes or to the eyes of others. I always wanted them to be stylish and beautiful."

From this grew a series of assemblages, "bits and pieces of former leg braces that I've saved over the years and at last I can celebrate their beauty and their importance in my life. This spiritual journey has been one of self-acceptance, beauty and celebration. I hope this series will encourage you to rediscover and challenge the 'braces' in your lives so that you, too, can celebrate your own beauty and empowerment."

Barbara Hardaway, now a full Professor of English at Gallaudet University, Washington, D.C., paints and exhibits outstanding and varied collages, writes poetry, and conducts workshops to help bridge the gap between the "impaired" (her word of choice) and the rest of the world. She has been the keynote speaker in many major programs for organizations and institutions, including Deaf Pride, the Association of Affirmative Action Professionals, the National Association of Equal Opportunities in Higher Education, Howard University and George Mason University. She has exhibited and sold her art in Washington, D.C., Maryland, Switzerland, and elsewhere.

As a child she grew up in a single-parent home in Roxbury, Massachusetts, where she was brought up by her mother with one brother and two sisters. All the children had polio in the 1955 epidemic, but hers was the worst case. She attended Cotting School for 12 years.

"As a child and young adult, I devalued myself," admits Barbara, "People's reactions to braces and crutches give a person a sense of poor self-esteem and often I felt like half a person. I received great support from

Cotting School. They did so much to make me feel I could succeed. I wanted to find a quality of life for myself at a young age. I've said to others in my imagination: 'your perception of me will <u>not</u> be my reality.' The quality of life was intrinsically bound up with building an appreciation of who I am and integrating this with my physical impairment. One had to work at feeling lovable as well as loved."

When Barbara's father remarried, her stepmother, Mattie, became an important role model. "She showed me by example how to respect myself and all human beings, and was an inspiration."

After she graduated from Cotting School, Barbara wanted to go to Boston University, but at that time B.U. had a rule that no one with an impairment of any kind could apply to the theater department. So she went, instead, to American International College in Springfield, Mass. where she took a B.A. in English and Sociology. Then she spent a year at the University of Ibadan in Nigeria, studying African theater and playwriting, and received a postgraduate diploma. After taking an M.A. from Emerson College in Boston, she did a year of postgraduate work at the University of Maryland. She earned a Ph.D. in Intercultural Communications at Howard University while studying sign language at Gallaudet University.

Throughout her academic career, Barbara was involved in many theatrical projects--as actor, director, set designer and playwright. She participated in productions in New York City; Atlanta, Georgia; Maryland; Talladega College, Alabama; and Roxbury Community College in Boston.

Barbara's employment record is equally varied. In the early 1970s she was an Assistant Lecturer in African-American Literature at the International College in Springfield. In the summers from 1974 through 1977 she was Instructor in English Composition and Afro-American Literature at Roxbury Community College; Assistant Professor of Drama and Public Speaking and Composition, as well as Director of the Performing Arts Program at Talladega College; then a teacher of speech at the University of Maryland, and finally, in the early 1980s, Supervisor/Counselor at the "C" Street Center for mentally impaired adults in Washington, D.C.

Since 1983 Barbara has been on the faculty in the English Department at Gallaudet University where she teaches Composition, African-American Literature and Multicultural Literature.

Barbara's career is not limited to teaching and art. She writes poetry and frequently participates in and leads workshops aimed at improving communication and understanding between stigmatized and nonstigmatized people. The title of one of her postgraduate publications, "We Are All Impaired" is the key to her workshop activity, as is her collected poetry, entitled "The House of Being Different." This highlights the idea that "as we become increasingly aware of the differences in our world, we are encouraged to explore the likenesses we all share." She is convinced that "people will accept other people to the extent that they accept themselves and their own vulnerabilities. It's a two-way street.

Impaired persons and those who appear nonimpaired are, at first, both apprehensive of one another and nervous about making real contact. The gap has to be bridged carefully and slowly.

In Barbara's opinion, everyone is impaired in one way or another and no one wants to confront this reality because of the discomfort we feel with the topic. One of her poems well expresses this first, uneasy feeling of non-rapport:

As I stood before Society's looking glass

My very own image was etched upon their faces.

Quizzical stares defining who I was.

Who I would become.

A mutual discomfort was the one thing

We shared.

I apologized.

And grew up avoiding my own mirrors. (1980)

Barbara has put particular emphasis on improving communication with deaf people. She observes: "once I got into deafness, so much of the communication is physical that I haven't missed the theater. I see this as an extension of my theater years. My teaching philosophy is; Meet me half way. I can't do my job if you don't do yours.' All really good teachers must be actors."

Barbara views students as the most honest audience there is. "I'm constantly aware that my students are looking at me and I have the responsibility to give them the gift of example. So my physically impaired students help me and my deaf students help me. We design tests together. We negotiate and problem solve. It's the personal, cooperative nature of teaching that I stress--the communication."

Because she is such a good communicator, Barbara is much in demand as a keynote speaker and presenter at workshops and conferences in different parts of the U.S.A. and other countries. She has recently been in New Jersey, Indiana, California, West Germany, Senegal and the Bahamas.

Partly due to her workshop activity, Barbara has become something of an expert on the correct use of language in dealing with people of all kinds. She insists that "disabled" is an incorrect term when used to refer to all impaired people, because it suggests a car that is broken down or a plane that has to make an emergency landing, something that is out of commission and cannot function. Injured athletes are put on the "disabled" list. "Handicapped" is equally incorrect because of its origin. Barbara reminds us that historically: "handicapped was the name of an old gambling game in which players threw forfeited money into a cap. Beggars who survived on the fringes of communities that had rejected them, became known as 'handicapped' because they lived with their 'caps in hand.' "

Socially disadvantaged, stigmatized by their poor social conditions, these handicapped outcasts were expected to beg in order to survive or to rely on the generosity of their families. The label "handicapped" remains today, along with the social rejection and inferior status that it connotes. Today, however, people with impairments are not automatically socially disadvantaged, quite the contrary for many. In Hardaway's opinion, everyone is impaired in one way or another; some happen to be stigmatized, while others are not. One of her poems expresses this well:

Definitions

There is a difference between

an inconvenienced traveler

a disabled traveler

and a normal traveler.

There is a difference between

Me

You

and Them.

Inconvenienced:

I move through life

w/impairments to guide me.

Disabled:

You have not grown

to trust your guide.

Together we live out our lives

attached to your labels.

Labels that secure separatism.

Labels that justify being Excluded.

Normaled:

They have yet to begin their journey

Unaware that universal sameness

Dwells in the 'House of Being Different.'

Hardaway sums up American society's treatment of persons with impairment conditions in two words: segregation and inequality. "Today persons with impairments are faced constantly with a wide array of psychological barriers, in addition to the physical barriers often alluded to in discussions of public accessibility. Although improvements are now being made in the areas of architectural and communicative accessibility...the barrier most difficult to dismantle is the attitudinal climate in this country that communicates an overt as well as covert rejection of people with any noticeable impairment condition."

On the other hand, referring to the accomplishments of ADA, she points out: "Remember that the United States is the only country in the world where concern for the impaired is legislated. At least an attempt has been made, even if imperfect. This country has made an awfully big statement. I can say, if I am badly treated: 'What you are doing is not just unkind, but illegal.' There are legal consequences and empowerment with ADA legislation. One must provide education and training to people to address discomfort and communication problems that exist. I don't get on my soap box too often, but try to use it well."

Barbara considers herself to be in "a privileged position--as a teacher established in her career, a person grounded in her spirituality and a respected practicing visual artist. I never wanted to be a starving artist! And now I don't have to be. I am fortunate; I can now do art for the sake of art. This is what brings me the greatest joy. But now I have a tremendous responsibility to acknowledge all the gifts I have been given. I have to be vigilant in using my talents purposefully to help others become aware of their own gifts."

Doctor Hardaway has published extensively and has received many awards. She has been honored as an Outstanding Young Woman in America and by Who's Who in America, as well as Who's Who in American Colleges and Universities. She received the Distinguished Alumna Award from Cotting School in 1994.

Barbara admits that she has "not yet found Mr. Right. I have a long list of frogs!" She has had several important relationships, some of them deep enough to inspire unusual love poetry, but is still seeking the person to complement her own enthusiastic, hopeful, talented personality.

This extraordinary professional person brings both to her teaching and her art a rare combination of depth and mischievous humor-- suggesting that life is both serious and yet full of madcap fun. Of her work as a visual artist, she says: "As a collage artist, I create fun and fantasy in mixed media and paper that celebrates life in an offbeat fashion.

Sometimes I show beauty in places where one might not expect it, and transform objects into artifacts that go beyond their intended use. I often move in directions of bold colors and contrasting elements to create visual tension and playful energy."

"Celebrate" is a word Barbara uses often, and it sums up her overall attitude to life. Asked about her religious views, she observes: "I am spiritual, not religious. I know that there is an order to the universe, a higher power. Look at the seasons, the sun, the moon, the sea. Look at individual talent. We can't explain all this in rational terms, so there must be a power greater than ourselves. I like rituals. I light a candle every morning. It burns throughout the day and when I put it out at night, I say: 'Thank you, God, for this day'. The ritual is my reminder to respect this life, every moment of it."

Barbara's candle is like her life--it throws a far-flung message. "How far that little candle sheds her beams--so shines a good deed in a naughty world."

# ACHIEVER AGAINST THE ODDS

## Ralf Hotchkiss

Ralf Hotchkiss
Inventor, Ambassador to the Third World

## ACHIEVER AGAINST THE ODDS

### Ralf Hotchkiss

Ralf Hotchkiss sits in his living room in a wheelchair of his own design, gazing out the window at the Pacific ocean and the view of the Farallon Islands, just visible on the horizon. His house in Oakland, California, is a busy place, where Ralf frequently talks into the night with guests from all over the world. Invariably they discuss improved wheelchair design for people far away. It is a home where dreams become reality.

Hotchkiss, who has been paralyzed from the chest down since a motorcycle accident in his freshman year of college, talks of faraway places such as Africa, South America and the Philippines. Places where there are no improved roads or sidewalks, let alone wheelchair ramps. In some cases, places where, until recently, there were no wheelchairs at all.

Hotchkiss does more than dream about these remote parts of the world where being disabled often means a life of isolation. He has visited most of them in person, journeying from village to village and stopping

47

at local blacksmiths if his specially-designed wheelchair is in need of repair. Often he and his friends camp out and cook meals on a tiny wood stove that fits in a pouch under his seat. He uses skills learned in his youth as a Boy Scout in Rockford, Illinois, as well as his hard-won experience in the intervening years. He hopes to share an African trek with his adopted son, Desmond, sometime in the future.

These have been unusual journeys, because Ralf Hotchkiss is an unusual man. A successful inventor, born in 1947, he is not merely a designer of wheelchairs, but a pioneer whose work has opened new horizons for disabled people in many parts of the Third World. He has traveled to dozens of countries including Nicaragua, Kenya, Mongolia and Sri Lanka, showing local blacksmiths and craftsmen how to build inexpensive wheelchairs that are strong enough to deal with primitive conditions, yet can be repaired cheaply and easily on the spot.

"To be disabled here, even in the lushest of surroundings, is not easy," he says. "Imagine a situation in which the disabled person lives at the end of an unpaved road, with no phone. She is making a living and raising children in the back country of Nicaragua or the slums of Nairobi. I have learned a great deal from people in such countries.

"Here at home, our need is usually not great enough to force us to design and build our own improved wheelchairs. In a Third World country, a person doesn't have an 800 number to call for parts, a credit card, or even a phone; she goes to the local blacksmith to get a new wheelchair frame and to the tailor to get upholstery. Often she redesigns in the process. Often the wheelchair becomes stronger, better and faster. When I met people solving their wheelchair problems by designing and building their own improvements, I knew I had found the people who could help me solve the problems I was having with my own wheelchair. This project has turned into a valuable partnership for all of us."

After his freshman year at Oberlin College, at home for summer vacation, Ralf recalls: "I went for a test spin on a motorbike at a summer picnic. I went too fast around the curve of a country road and skidded out of control." At age 18, Hotchkiss was paralyzed for good.

At the time, he was majoring in physics. His long-range ambition, written on his college application, was to become a designer of devices for people with disabilities. Because of his accident, he believes he has become a better engineer, much more sensitive to the needs of the people who will depend on his product for their mobility. "I might have been just like many rehab engineers and followed solutions that real disabled people don't ask for," he says.

Hotchkiss took a year off school after his accident, three months of which he spent in a rehabilitation center in Chicago. He had been working in a summer factory program, which trained engineers, as part of his college course. "The factory was great," he recalls. "It gave me moral support, sent me work in the hospital, and encouraged me to get back to work as fast as possible."

While he was at the rehab center, Hotchkiss wrote at length to James Leeson, a physicist and mechanical engineer whom he considered his best technical teacher at the factory. He received an encouraging letter in return, exchanging ideas about design and urging him to pursue his intended career. Shortly after he returned to college, he was invited to co-author a book with Ralph Nader called What to Do with a Bad Car, which soon became known across the country as "the lemon book." Hotchkiss wrote the mechanical chapters, explaining how a car works and breaks.

Ralf Hotchkis' own career is expanding rapidly. "Thirty years ago, I began experimenting with new design for wheelchairs," he says. "Now I get ideas from a network of people all over the world. I make at least three trips every year out of the U.S.A. visiting developing countries."

He finds that work in Third World countries is inspiring, yet grueling. It all started by coincidence when he visited Nicaragua in 1980 and was told to bring his tools. There he found four people, two of them expert mechanics, sharing one chair. Over the next three years, working with 16-year-old Nicaraguan student, Omar Talavera (who later attended the University of California at Berkeley and became an engineer for NASA in Silicon Valley), Ralf designed and built a wheelchair--the "Whirlwind"--which could be assembled locally for $140. Thelma Ayala, a wheelchair builder in Nicaragua's Independent Living Center, rode the first Whirlwind to victory in the 1983 Managua Wheelchair Marathon.

"Her victory shocked the city," Hotchkiss recalled later, "and the

Managua men, their machismo bruised by the loss to a woman, flooded the Center with orders."

In 1981, Hotchkiss and his Nicaraguan friend journeyed to the Philippines. They visited a group of Filipino wheelchair riders who were making copies of expensive imported chairs. "The price for an import was $1,000, but they sold them there for $150," Hotchkiss recalls. "In the islands at that time it took 21 person-days to build one chair, so the $150 sale price was a complete loss for the builder. We had to develop more sophisticated designs for the frames and other parts. We eventually worked the time down from 21 to five person-days to make a wheelchair. The Philippine group taught me a lot, more than any American source."

A few years later, Hotchkiss travelled to Atoya, the remote Mexican village, where the widely used health manual Where There Is No Doctor was written. This village is 20 miles from the nearest road and telephone. Here he organized their first start-up operation to build wheelchairs from readily available materials. "I was learning all the time," he recalls. "The chairs got better and better. By this time, dozens of people, some with no formal education, had made significant contributions to the design of the chair."

His work at home went hand in hand with research and achievements abroad. At the instigation of Professor Peter Pfaelzer, Ralf Hotchkiss began teaching at San Francisco State University in 1985; soon after that he co-founded the Rehabilitation Engineering Project and the

Wheeled Mobility Center at SFSU with Professor Pfaelzer. Since then he has continued to teach the wheelchair design and building courses at SFSU. Students from many developing countries assist him at the University and thus acquire the knowledge to carry on the work in their own lands. Partly as an extension of his work in Third World countries, Hotchkiss and Pfaelzer together obtained a grant to start the Wheeled Mobility Center-- this was accomplished by a lot of persistent hard work. The Wheeled Mobility Center (WMC) is now world famous.

Hotchkiss is also an advocate for better telecommunications for people with disabilities. "New systems will be on line in a few years that have the capability to improve life for all of us," he says, "but they may be too poorly or too hastily designed. People will be whizzing through technology, to try to beat the competition, but not thinking of the implications for people like us. We must make sure that disabled people are kept in mind."

Hotchkiss remains Technical Director of the Center and teaches the wheelchair building courses. The Center is dedicated to "creating wheeled technology that maximizes the quality of life for people with disabilities throughout the world." Hotchkiss has become a goodwill ambassador for the U.S. through his wheelchair mission.

Between 1980 and 1997, the Wheeled Mobility Center helped to start more than 35 wheelchair building workshops in 25 developing countries. "The workshops are usually led by skilled technicians who are themselves wheelchair riders," Hotchkiss explains. "More than 150 mechanics have been trained and well over ten thousand wheelchairs have been produced."

This accomplishment is the direct result of Hotchkiss' obsession to build a wheelchair "that was simpler and better." In Nicaragua, Zimbabwe, Mexico, Jamaica, India and the Philippines, he went to primitive workshops and talked with people who make carts, buggies, rickshaws, bicycles and wheelchairs. With the advice of these craftspeople he has designed a wheelchair with only 125 parts (as opposed to 250 in many commercially made chairs) that can be built and maintained with basic tools in developing countries worldwide. He has also written a training manual for his Whirlwind Wheelchair, titled <u>Independence Through Mobility;</u> this has been translated into Spanish and distributed all over the world.

Wheelchair riders in Thailand, Estonia, Zimbabwe, Fiji, Mexico, Kenya, Nigeria, Jamaica, India, Malawi, Paraguay, Sri Lanka, Russia and many other countries have benefited from Hotchkiss' industry and expertise.

"The poorer countries MUST make their own wheelchairs, because wheelchairs imported to developing countries have been difficult or impossible to repair. Most of these wheelchairs are ill-suited to the rough urban and rural environments of developing countries."

<u>"This work is not about good guys giving to the poor,"</u> Ralf

stresses. He and his team have succeeded in getting inventors in the industrialized world and Third World countries to collaborate to build better wheelchairs. Members of the Whirlwind Network are continuing to come up with solutions useful to people with disabilities all over the world.

Two of the more impressive tributes come from Russia. "Since Wheeled Mobility came to us in Novosibirsk in 1993, it's like we've been awakened from a deep sleep," said Arina Arnatova. "I was imprisoned in my apartment for 32 years," added Valentina Fedorvona Kusnestova. "Now, thanks to WMC, I have a good wheelchair and a new life."

In 1989, Hotchkiss was awarded a $260,000 grant and named a fellow of the MacArthur Foundation, a national program that honors people for excellence in their field. In 1994, he received the Henry B. Betts Award for improving the lives of people with disabilities. Despite these honors and the fact that the Wheeled Mobility Center now has an international, multilingual staff that conducts clinics all over the globe, Hotchkiss is modest about himself and his achievements. "Publicity is not my goal," he emphasizes, "just freedom for myself and others."

Hotchkiss credits the Americans With Disabilities Act (ADA) with giving businesses and public institutions a new focus on their responsibilities toward disabled people. "This is not just an act of charity," he points out. "It is required. The same people who might have provided reasonable access without ADA are now doing a lot more, providing 'greater access,' whereas those who would have done nothing before this law at least have to make some minimal effort."

His advice to people with new disabilities: "Find somebody with the same disability as yours who can give you good advice. There are plenty of people out there who'll be quick to befriend you. Better still, find someone with a more significant disability than your own, who will convince you not to pity them. This will help you deal with your <u>own</u> perception of loss."

Hotchkiss admits that, although as a child he knew people with disabilities, he had prejudices of his own against them. After his injury, he didn't want to date people with disabilities, "because I was afraid to be pushed into that category and kept there."

Concerned about perceived links between religion and people with disabilities, Hotchkiss believes that some have held the view that people become disabled as a punishment for sinning, looking on injury as just retribution.

"One of the goals of the Disability Rights Movement is to excise guilt for sin as a view of why people become disabled," he explains. "I am myself a Unitarian, a religious liberal. I have to deal with this in my own life. For nearly 20 years after my accident, I didn't belong to any organized church." Ralf Hotchkiss is passionately opposed to 'Retribution Theology'--the fear that disabled people are being justly punished for something they have done. "This is a 400-year-old, narrow-minded error on the part of the theologians," he maintains. "It was used to justify the

55

imprisonment of people with disabilities in isolated work camps. Sheltered workshops originally meant 'sheltered' from the temptations of sin. The issue has become somewhat blurred in recent times, taken off the table of discussion as it were. But the prejudice is alive and well." Hotchkiss actively campaigns against what he sees as a current tendency to "sweep the whole issue under the rug."

This remarkable inventor is descended from a long line of independently minded people. In the 1630s, two brothers left England in the years just preceding the English Civil War when religious dissension and opposition to King Charles I were at their height. The Hotchkiss brothers settled in what eventually became Connecticut, and, in the early 19th century, one of their descendants, a pioneer inventor, constructed a wheelchair that was pulled around Sharon, Connecticut, by a dog.

Hotchkiss may prefer to shun the limelight, but plenty of publicity has come his way regardless. In December 1996, he was "Person of the Week" on one of Peter Jennings' ABC international nightly newscasts. In February 1997, he was profiled on Tom Brokaw's NBC Nightly News. This program traced Hotchkiss' career from his early days as a promising physics student, to the accident that left him paralyzed, to his present revolutionary designs for inexpensive, easy to build wheelchairs for disabled people in poor nations throughout the world. "These are the experiences that make life worth living," said Hotchkiss. "To be with somebody when he goes into his own front yard for the first time in his life and moves under his own power...this wheelchair represents freedom, his freedom."

In 1995, Hotchkiss was one of six recipients of the Chrysler Award for Innovation in Design, and in April 1997, he was inducted into the San Francisco State University Alumni Hall of Fame, selected by a student-faculty committee of SFSU to receive the "Achievers Against the Odds" Award for "vision, innovative achievements and dedication to providing independent living for people with disabilities."

Ralf Hotchkiss remains more concerned about the future than the past. The design of the new wheelchair that will someday cross Africa will call not only on all his own skills, but also the accumulated knowledge of hundreds of others. "We will be dealing with a largely unpaved continent," he says. "We must design a chair that will be equal to it, that will cross rough terrain, that will work well in tiny outhouses...we plan to have a few 'rehearsals' on shorter trips first."

At the same time, Hotchkiss pursues a grander vision: "the dream of seeing 20 million wheelchairs produced in developing countries around the world by the year 2020."

"Ralf Hotchkiss may be the ultimate altruist," wrote Time Magazine in 1992. "[He's] an inventor who refuses to patent his ideas because he wants to share them with people in need throughout the world....he has devoted his adult life to helping the disabled 'become actively integrated into schools, regular jobs, places to live and public life....'

"Students from all over the world come to San Francisco to learn how to build wheelchairs practical enough and inexpensive enough for use back home.... Hotchkiss designed a wheelchair that can be assembled in the Third World for about $140...each one, thanks to Ralf Hotchkiss, gives a gift most of us take for granted--mobility--to people who may never have had it before."

This new mobility has altered the view that many people, especially Third World people, may have of Americans as greedy, opportunistic capitalists and little more. In applying his intelligence and tenacity to improving his own life, Hotchkiss has altered the lives of thousands of others all over the world, creating living testimonials to the strength of one man's vision and determination.

Time Magazine celebrated Ralf Hotchkiss as an "Amazing American." But disabled people all over the world already knew that. He has most certainly lifted our nation's pride in distant places where it most counts.

## "GO FOR BROKE!!"

**Daniel K. Inouye, U.S. Senator From Hawaii**

The Honorable Daniel K. Inouye
U.S. Senator from Hawaii

## "GO FOR BROKE!!"

### Daniel K. Inouye, U.S. Senator From Hawaii

The date was Thursday, August 23, 1959 and the House of Representatives, although filled to capacity, was very still. It was about to witness one of the most dramatic and moving scenes ever to occur there—the swearing in, not only of the first Congressman from Hawaii, but the first American of Japanese descent ever to serve as a member of Congress.

On that day, a young man, just elected to Congress from the brand-new state of Hawaii, walked into the well of the House and stood before Speaker Sam Rayburn.

"Raise your right hand and repeat after me," said the Speaker.

The hush deepened as the young Congressman raised not his right hand but his left, and repeated the oath of office.

"There was no right hand," Congressman Leo O'Brien recalled later. "It had been lost in combat by that young American soldier in World War II...at that moment, a ton of prejudice slipped quietly to the

61

floor of the House of Representatives." [1]

The young man was Daniel Ken Inouye, a war hero with the 442nd Regimental Combat Team, whose political career on Capitol Hill would span more than four decades. It would not take long for his colleagues in the House and Senate to discover that he considered the challenges of prejudice and bigotry far more important than getting along without his right arm.

Soon after his swearing in, Inouye received a telephone call from Rayburn, inviting him to his office. As a newcomer to Washington, Inouye was suitably impressed by the Speaker's personal interest. As they chatted in Rayburn's office, Inouye admitted to being "very proud and very happy and a little scared." [2] Rayburn assured him that everyone felt this way in their first term.

Then the Speaker got to the point. "Now, Dan, I'm sure you know that I am the best-known member of the House of Representatives."

"Yes, sir."

"Well, after me, do you know who the best-known member is?"

"No."

"You."

"Me?" I looked at him with astonishment. Was he pulling my leg?

"Of course, you," he said in that flat, no-nonsense way he had. "Oh, maybe not this very minute, not today. But very damned soon."

"But-why?"

"Why? Well, just think about it, son. How many one-arm Japanese do you think we have in the Congress of the United States?" [3]

Inouye considered Rayburn to be "one of the great Americans of the 20th century. Apart from his towering skills of statesmanship, he had an infinite regard for people..." [4] They remained friends until Rayburn's death in 1961. [5]

The background to this dramatic encounter in Washington, in 1959, took place in 1945 when Inouye was less than 20 years old. As a member of the "Go For Broke" 442nd Regimental Combat Team, the famous Nisei regiment of Japanese- Americans, Sergeant Inouye slogged through nearly three months of the Rome-Arno campaign with the U.S. Fifth Army. Early in the action, he established himself as an outstanding patrol leader, often given some of the most dangerous assignments.

Inouye's unit was shifted to the French Vosges Mountains, where it spent two of the bloodiest weeks of the war rescuing a Texas Battalion surrounded by German forces. The rescue of 'The Lost Battalion' is listed in the U.S. Army annals as one of the most significant military battles of the century. Inouye lost ten pounds, became a platoon leader, won the Bronze Star and a battlefield commission as Second Lieutenant. [6]

Less than a month later, on April 21st, Inouye led the attack that cost him his right arm. Back in Italy, the 442nd was assaulting a heavily defended hill in the closing months of the war when Lieut. Inouye was hit in his abdomen by a bullet which came out his back, barely missing his spine. He continued to lead the platoon and advanced alone against a machine gun nest which had his men pinned down.

He tossed two hand grenades with devastating effect before his right arm was shattered by a German rifle grenade at close range. Inouye threw his last grenade with his left hand, attacked with a submachine gun, and was finally knocked down the hill by a bullet in the leg. [7]

He refused to leave the battlefield until his whole platoon arrived, and he held on to his own artery until a medic finally managed to get a tourniquet around what was left of his arm. He was carried down the hill on a litter. When he finally arrived at the battalion aid station, so much morphine had been given him on the battlefield that the first treatments had to be endured with little anesthetic. [8]

"...Hours and whole days are lost in some dark void where I drifted with parched lips and a constant feeling of nausea and wildly-colored dreams of exploding grenades....the raw truth was that the things they were doing to my arm hurt so badly that dying didn't seem like such an awful idea..." [9]

This episode was undoubtedly the worst memory Inouye has of World War II.

After 20 months of rehabilitation in Army hospitals, he came home as a Captain with a Distinguished Service Cross (the second highest award for military valor), Bronze Star, Purple Heart with Cluster and 12 other medals and citations. He also came home with an attitude: "There wasn't a thing in the world I couldn't do with my left hand, if I wanted to do it badly enough.[10]

"Like all who experience extreme trauma, I spent my share of moments depressed with the turn of events," he said. "However, I got over it fast. I soon learned that there were not too many others who felt sorry for me. I realized that if I did not help myself, no one else would. I have accepted my injury as a lifetime challenge. I believe I have succeeded. [11]

"Life has been good, but it has been tough. The loss of my right arm has never been an insurmountable obstacle or impediment against the attainment of the goals I have set for myself." [12]

"On April 21, 1945...I was 20 years old with dreams of returning to college to become an orthopedic surgeon," he recalled. "The initial impact of my injuries [on Mount Marchiaso] was one of self-pity. It soon became apparent that I would never be an orthopedic surgeon nor would I ever play my favorite ukulele, but as the months progressed, it became clear to me that I was indeed very fortunate. I not only returned home, but before doing so, a great nation—the United States of America—provided me with the best of medical care and finest rehabilitation program. In addition, with the extraordinary program called the GI Bill of Rights, I was able to continue my college education and receive my Juris Doctor

Degree in Law.

"I am certain that this experience has made me a better person than that young man of 18, who left Hawaii in an ill-fitting uniform on a morning in March 1943. My gratitude to my nation can never be repaid." [13]

Inouye's 20 months in hospitals and rehab centers had a marked effect on shaping his later career. In groups where Italians, Irish, Jews, Poles and other ethnic groups tended to band together, he was often the only Nisei. He came to have great sympathy and respect for black soldiers who were invariably in the minority and received little respect. [14]

As President Lyndon Johnson was to say of him later: "Daniel K. Inouye...is one of America's great egalitarians. [His life] reflects his relentless struggle to achieve freedom of opportunity and equality for Americans of Japanese [descent] and for all racial and religious minorities. [15]

"Dan Inouye has lived by the code of personal courage—on the battlefield, and in the political arena. He has faced the aggressor's bullets, and the bigot's contemptuous stare. He has gained the admiration and respect of his fellow men. Even more important, he has, by his example and witness, helped to make the hearts of his fellow men more tolerant, more free of the awful burden of racism." [16]

The seeds to pursue this crusade later in the halls of Congress were sown in the 442nd and during his association with wounded men after his last battle. "For the first time," he observed, "I really came to understand haoles [Caucasians] as people. I mean, let's face it, you eat and sleep and learn with a bunch of guys,and help change the dressings on their amputated arms and legs, and pretty soon you don't even notice that their eyes are shaped differently from yours. What you do notice is that they're people, the same as you are, with a set of worries and joys that pretty well match your own." [17]

Inouye was thinking during these months about his future. He knew that his long dream of becoming a surgeon was no longer possible and speculated that he would like to work with people in some useful capacity. In the meantime, he played basketball, learned to drive, played a one-handed "Danny Boy" on the piano, and showed a talent for gambling. [18] When one of his greatest friends, Sake Takahashi, left to go into law school, Inouye began to contemplate becoming a lawyer himself.[19] It helped that "over the next 20 months this bristle-edged, roughneck of an infantry officer was transformed into something resembling a gentleman....You might even say that by washing the grime from my poor boy's face and straightening my nisei necktie, they made it possible for me to think seriously about trying for political office," he said. [20]

When he finally returned to Honolulu, his mother was surprised: "This is what you learned in the war? To talk like a haole and behave like a gentleman?" [21] She was even more appalled when he lit a cigarette. "...Mother came to her feet as though pinched. 'Daniel Ken Inouye!' she said in exactly the old way....we all began to laugh, my mother too, and I knew that I was home." [22]

Inouye was born in Honolulu on September 7, 1924, in a house on Queen Emma Street where "two-family houses pressed one on the other and a street full of children [screeched] a piercing...jangle of Japanese and English." [23] His grandfather and grandmother had emigrated from Japan many years previously, to earn money to pay a $400 family debt of honor (a staggering sum in those days) [24] by working on a sugar plantation. They took with them their four-year old son, Hyotaro, who was to become Daniel's father.[25]

Hyotaro and his Japanese-born wife, Kame, were poor people, and brought up their family with extreme frugality. Daniel remembers his mother dividing a single egg among six people for breakfast and took this as a matter of course throughout his boyhood. [26]

Young Inouye attended Honolulu public schools and earned pocket money by parking cars at the old Honolulu Stadium, and giving haircuts to fellow students. Most of his earnings were spent on a flock of homing pigeons, a postage stamp collection, parts for a crystal radio, and chemistry sets.[27] In his teens, he supplemented his income by helping tourists learn to surf at Waikiki Beach. [28]

Inouye's grandmother, Moyo, died of cancer, and young Daniel was so impressed with Doctor Sato, who cared for her at home in her final months, he decided to become a doctor himself when he grew up. He began to read books on medicine at the Library of Hawaii. "...my parents encouraged me," he said. "To have a doctor in the family was the absolute peak of achievement to which a Japanese household could aspire...." [29]

As part of this long-range ambition, he enrolled in a Red Cross First Aid course and after he received his certificate, began to teach courses of his own. [30]

By December 7, 1941, when Pearl Harbor was bombed, 17-year old Daniel Inouye was one of the first Americans to handle civilian casualties in the Pacific war. By then he had enough medical aid training to be pressed into service as head of a first-aid litter team. He saw "a lot of blood" and did not go home for a week. [31]

For more than a year he worked the night shift as a medical aide at the First Aid Center and went to school in the daytime, sleeping only in short snatches. He earned $125 a month. [32] However, in spite of his war work, he was well aware of "the full and bitter burden shared by every one of the 158,000 Japanese Americans in Hawaii. Not only had our country been wantonly attacked, but our loyalty was...called into question...there would always be those who would look at us and think— and some would say it aloud: 'Dirty Jap.' " [33]

The full force of this came home to the Inouye family when a shortwave radio, purchased by Dan's father after careful saving, and much prized by the family, was seized and destroyed by police officers. [34] A bitter blow.

Surprisingly, in the face of this treatment, Inouye and his friends were relentless in their efforts to be allowed to enlist in the U.S. Army and, "...despite every derogation and disparagement, Japanese-Americans fought for a place in the war effort, no matter how small or menial. Older men, including my father, organized their own labor squads, and volunteered for garbage details and ditch-digging." [35] President Roosevelt recognized the loyalty of Japanese-Americans when he said: "Americanism is a matter of the mind and heart; Americanism is not, and never was, a matter of race or ancestry." [36]

Largely because of Roosevelt's backing, a year after Pearl Harbor, the War Department announced that it would accept "4,000 nisei volunteers to form a full-fledged combat team for front-line service without restriction, without restraints."[37]  When this news was announced, Inouye with many others, raced to the draft board, and, because of his speed, he arrived among the first 75. [38] However, because he was by then enrolled as a pre-med student at the University of Hawaii, and medical service was considered indispensable, he had trouble persuading the authorities to accept him as an enlisted man. He was, as ever, persistent in his requests, and, "of the 2,686 members of the Hawaiian-Japanese of the 442nd Regimental Combat Team, I was No. 2,685." [39] His father's message to him the day before he sailed was:

"[America] has been good to us...and now ...it is you who must try to return the goodness of this country...do not bring dishonor on our name!" [40]

During the next three years, Inouye certainly lived up to his father's charge. From Camp Shelby in Mississippi, where, "without any fooling around we began those thirteen long, hard months of training that would make us soldiers," [41] and throughout his wartime experience, Inouye exemplified the courage of the Japanese-Americans. As one of his commanders, Captain Ralph B. Ensminger, a man he much admired, pointed out: "You men have an additional battle to fight. You have to overcome the prejudice and discrimination that has been thrown at you, because your forefathers came from a country that is now our enemy....What can you do about it? First, you can be the best damn soldiers this country has ever known. You can fight your first battle with everything you've got. And, second, you can conduct yourselves with the honor for which your people have been known." [42]

Inouye and the men he led did just this. His prayer before his first battle was simple: "Please God, let me do what must be done." [43] He was promoted rapidly and wondered at one point "why the C.O. had chosen to entrust the fate of 1,000 fighting men to a nineteen-year-old buck sergeant." [44]

The reason soon became clear. Inouye was respected by his men and kept his head. "I didn't believe in volunteers. That might work

71

gloriously for John Wayne and Errol Flynn. But when the bullets are real, the men you want backing you up on a dangerous mission are the ones...with a healthy appreciation of the odds, a sensible respect for the enemy, and a rational concern for [their] own [lives]." [45] Despite this "rational concern," the 442nd had one of the highest casualty rates and lowest AWOL rates of any unit in the European Theater of Operations. [46]

Shortly after he was made a Second Lieutenant, Inouye commanded a group which captured Mount Folgorito, taking the Germans by complete surprise. "Barely forty-eight hours had elapsed since the commanding general had asked if we could do the job in a week—and this over terrain that had stymied the best efforts of Allied troops for fully five months." [47] This sort of swift action characterized Inouye's military career. Less than a month later, on April 21 1945, Inouye led the attack which cost him his right arm.

"This is an American story," Vice President Hubert Humphrey was to write later. "Dan's boyhood in Honolulu really was not so different from mine in South Dakota. He had the ocean and I had the prairie. But we both had the great gift of discovering that there is no limit to the aspirations of an American boy. His father worked in a jewelry store and my father was a druggist. We both learned that in this land of ours a man's beginnings are not nearly so important as his hope for the future..." [48]

Inouye arrived back in Hawaii at a fortuitous time. After WWII a political revolution was brewing, change was in the air and "it was an exciting time to be alive." [49]

The Army had given Inouye and his comrades a taste of full citizenship and an appetite for more of the same. "We were the 'can do' outfit and we were heady with a sense of ourselves," he recalled. "All those medals and citations proved something, didn't they?....if you were young in Hawaii in that pivotal year, if you were ambitious and believed implicitly in...the Declaration of Independence, what did it matter that you had only one arm? You had given it for America, and America, at last, was yours." [50]

Young Inouye's first venture into public life was the "battle of the crosses." Veterans were returned home to be buried in the Punch Bowl Cemetery in Honolulu, and it had been decided by those in authority that each grave would be marked with a cross. Inouye campaigned for each man to have his own symbol: a cross for Christians, a Star of David for Jews, a wheel for Buddhists, and nothing for nonbelievers.

Inouye was forced to defend his views to the local council of churches, and won his battle for appropriate individual symbols on each man's grave and thereafter frequently visited his friends in Punch Bowl on nonpublic days.[51]

Soon after this episode, in the summer of 1947, Inouye joined the Democratic Party and worked for Jack Burns, a former Police Captain, who was running as a delegate to the Territorial Congress to back the issue of statehood for Hawaii. Inouye greatly admired Burns, largely because he had been one of the few to stand up for Japanese-Americans and their loyalty when World War II broke out. [52]

Politics in Hawaii was then dominated by wealthy Republicans, a few Caucasian families whose ancestors had originally developed **the** islands' commerce a century before and continued to control the economy, but this was about to change. Although Inouye admits that the veterans of the 442nd were not politically savvy, after he was elected to the Board of the Veterans Club, he made sure that Burns, as well as Farrington, his old-guard Republican opponent, had a chance to speak.

Burns lost the election [53] but the Democratic Party was established in the islands, as was Inouye's personal political view about party differences: "The difference between them is that the Republicans' chief concern is property, things, what we own; the Democrats worry about people—what we are." [54]

In this same year Inouye met Margaret Awamura and conducted a whirlwind courtship. "Suddenly everything I had and wanted to have became absolutely meaningless unless Margaret would share it with me." He asked her to marry him on their second date and she accepted. [55] It was the start of a long and successful life's partnership.

"Our life was full, but not placid. Politics became an integral part of it, almost from the day we returned from our honeymoon. I went to weekly political meetings, meetings that went on for hour after interminable hour, and came tip-toeing at two or three in the morning. I don't say it was fair, but Maggie understood, bless her, that for me it was necessary." [56] Maggie realized that politics was rapidly becoming her husband's chief interest.

In 1950 Inouye graduated from the University of Hawaii and decided to apply to study law. He was accepted at George Washington University, Harvard, Columbia and Michigan law schools. He opted for George Washington University because he wanted to be in D.C., at the heart of government. He and his wife sailed for the mainland on the same ship that, eight years before, took him to America as an enlisted soldier.

During his years at the University of Hawaii and also during his time as a law student at George Washington University, Margaret Inouye not only wholeheartedly backed her husband's legal and political aspirations, but also played a practical role as a co-breadwinner to supplement Inouye's income from the G.I. Bill, his Army pension of $200 a month and various part-time jobs. They lived first in a boarding house in Washington, and then in a small apartment in Arlington, Virginia. [57]

After some of his briefs were published by the Law Review, Inouye was invited to join Phi Delta Phi, an international legal fraternity. After he had been there a few months, he persuaded the other members to elect two brilliant Jewish men as members, threatening to resign himself if they did not. "You see, I'm not an Anglo-Saxon and if these men don't belong in this fraternity, neither do I." [58]

Inouye not only worked hard at his courses, but served as a volunteer at the Democratic National Committee Headquarters where he quickly earned a reputation as a hard worker and fast learner; in his final year, he also spent a great deal of time in the Congressional galleries.

Inouye graduated in 1952 with a J.D. degree. His mother flew to Washington for the occasion. Then Maggie, Inouye, and classmate John Ushijama drove across country to the west coast, seeing, for the first time, New England, the plains of Iowa and Kansas, the desert, the mountains and the coast. "Never before had I really understood the immensity and diversity and great promise of this land of ours." [59]

In the year after his return from Washington, Inouye simultaneously studied for his upcoming bar examination and helped to organize a new bank to assist aspiring young businessmen, many of them of Japanese-American ancestry, to get started after the war. In both efforts he was successful. The bank application, after some months of argument and negotiation, was finally approved, and in August, Inouye learned that he had passed the Territorial Bar Exam. [60]

However, he did not have a chance to "hang out a shingle." The day after he passed the bar exam, Mayor Johnny Wilson, one of a handful of exceptional Democrats to succeed at the polls, called Inouye into his office and appointed him assistant prosecutor for the city and county of Honolulu. He recalled "I knew then, as I know now, that as long as I could walk, as long as I could talk, and as long as people wanted me, I was in politics to stay...I took charge of my first case that very afternoon." [61]

In 1954 Jack Burns ran for Territorial Delegate and Inouye became his campaign chairman. During the summer, Inouye himself was persuaded to run as senator from the 4th District. Dan Aoki, who was President of the Veterans Club and had been a First Sergeant in the 442nd, urged: "They'll go for you, Dan....you've got the right combination—a war hero, a fresh face. If we want the vets to come into the Democratic Party, we've got to give them somebody they care about, one of their own. You." [62]

As part of a six-person team from the 4th District, Inouye worked hard. At one debate, he routed his Republican opponent, who had accused the Democrats of being communists, by saying: "...I cannot help wondering whether the people of Hawaii will not think it strange that the only weapon in the Republican arsenal is to label as communists men so recently returned from defending liberty on the firing lines in Italy and France. Let me speak for those of us who didn't come back-I know I speak for my colleagues on this platform...when I say that we bitterly resent having our loyalty and patriotism questioned by cynical political hacks who lack the courage to debate the real issues in this campaign.

"I had never before called attention to my disability for the simple reason I didn't consider it a qualification for public office. But at that moment, blinded with fury...I held up my empty right sleeve and shook it. 'I gave this arm to fight fascists. If my country wants the other one to fight communists, it can have it!' " [63] Crashing applause.

Due to the efforts of Inouye and the rest of the team, Republican control of the Territorial Legislature was crumbling. When the votes were counted in the fall of 1954, the Democrats had won 22 of the 30 seats in the House and 10 of 15 in the Senate besides gaining control of most of the city and county councils. [64]

When Inouye was made Majority Leader, [65] he had the good sense to write for advice to Speaker Sam Rayburn. "And bless Mr. Sam's big Texas heart, he took sympathetic notice of this obscure Hawaiian legislator, of whom he had never heard, and whose name he wouldn't learn to pronounce for six years, and told me that, although the rules of legislative bodies differed...a majority leader had few constitutional powers...the post was a convenience and a tool to keep the legislative business moving....What then makes a good majority leader? The understanding, appreciation and practice of good human relations...the Golden Rule was as good a guide as he'd ever encountered. I don't think I have ever had better advice...." [66]

Simultaneously, Jack Burns, as Hawaii's Delegate to the U.S. Congress, was working for the admission of Hawaii as a state in the United States. This was opposed by many of the old-guard Republicans in Hawaii itself and by many in the Congress. The real reason was neither numbers nor dollars but the fact that much of Hawaii's population was non-Caucasian and, in fact, heavily Japanese. Alaska was also seeking statehood.

At the last minute Burns had the political wisdom to withdraw Hawaii at that time to give Alaska "a clear shot at it." Alaska became the

49th state. "With Alaska in, all the phony arguments about non-contiguity, population, and economy were undercut....in March 1959, the U.S. Congress voted to accept Hawaii as the 50th state. [67]

In an emotional aftermath to statehood, Inouye ran for the House of Representatives in Washington. When informed that he had won, Inouye told the press: "I would hope that my service in the Congress would be a bridge between the western world and the Orient. I would like to convey to the Mainland some small sense of our spirit of aloha..." [68]

A few days later Inouye "walked alone, among the graves of the good men with whom I had served. I wanted to assure them that I would not let them down, never dishonor the cause and the country for which they had given so much. I wanted to promise them that I was not going to Washington to represent the 442nd, or the Nisei, or any other separate group. I was going to represent all the people of Hawaii, and I asked God's help in this, the greatest undertaking of my life." [69]

Inouye was present on August 21, 1959, in the Oval Room of the White House, to witness the signing of the document which officially proclaimed Hawaii a state. Present were President Eisenhower, Vice President Nixon, Speaker Sam Rayburn and newly-elected Representative from Hawaii, Inouye. Jack Burns, for some petty political reason, had not been invited. Also present was a collection of pens to be presented to the participants. Despite his very junior status in the gathering, Inouye whispered to Rayburn about Burns' absence and

Rayburn requested a pen from the President to give to Burns later. [70]

In 1960, Inouye won re-election to Congress by the greatest number of votes ever polled by a candidate in the islands. During his second term, he was invited to serve on the American delegation to the Interparliamentary Union, the oldest such organization in the world, meeting in Tokyo that year. [71]

He flew from Tokyo to the old family village of Yokoyama and was welcomed like a returning hero, the first of his family to return in generations. Inouye's granduncle, now the head of the family, officially greeted him and escorted him around. People "were impressed, I later learned, not so much that I was an American Congressman, but because I was a member of a family [in which] all four children had gone to college, and because I had risen to an officer's rank in the Army...perhaps most important of all, I was an Inouye, a name that would always represent the highest honor in this valley because of the heroic lengths two generations had gone to [in order] to pay a debt." [72]

Inouye ceremonially visited the graves of his ancestors and won even more approval from the people of the village for knowing the correct procedure to be followed by a long-absent, eldest son. He was presented a samurai sword when he departed. [73]

The visit to Yokoyama brought back memories of the Inouye family, his grandparents and his parents. His pride in his background was and has remained strong. "Both [my parents] were ever willing to sacrifice for the sake of the children. My father...held two jobs, one during the day and one in the evening. His only day of rest was Sunday, the Sabbath. He never had a vacation. As the eldest son in his family, he felt that he was morally obligated to provide sustenance and shelter not only for his wife and children but also for his parents and his younger siblings. He never complained. He carried out his responsibilities with great dignity and much humor." [74] The elder Inouye was forced to retire after his second heart attack.

"My mother, although she never finished high school, was a learned person. She was an avid reader, always reading in those moments late at night after all her chores had been concluded. She was a great teacher, who dedicated her life to instilling in me the importance of honor, duty, loyalty and responsibility." [75]

Inouye's mother, Kame, who had been adopted and largely brought up by a Methodist minister, did not let Daniel forget he was of Oriental descent, and would say: "I take from the old ways what I think is good and useful. I take from the new ways what is good and useful. Anyone would be foolish not to."[76] Although my mother was a devout Christian, she always remembered the very early lessons of Buddhism, which she often shared with me." [77]

The Inouye family placed a great value on the importance of education. "When I began school, my father and mother began to speak only English at home...a hardship and a sacrifice and a great personal wrench for them...the most striking demonstration of how far the Inouye family had traveled since my grandfather set out on that long road from Yokoyama village just 25 years before..." [78]

Kame Inouye's influence on Daniel was great. She taught him, among other important lessons, that " 'there is no one who is too good for you....but remember, too, that there is a difference between pride and arrogance, for you are no better than anyone else either.' I...have never forgotten that little talk. In all the years to come it would help me to feel comfortable in the company of presidents and longshoremen, among people whose skin was white, brown, black or yellow." [79]

"Because of my mother's guidance I went into the workplace with much confidence and it is something that has not abandoned me in all these years. There are always challenges whether they be physical or intellectual, political or personal, But the greatest are moral challenges. [80]

"I do not consider myself disabled or crippled or physically challenged. I believe I can do just about everything a normal [...] person can do," said Inouye. "However, admittedly, I cannot embrace a person I love with both arms." [81]

"I am constantly greeted by people who exclaim with some shock: 'I did not know that you only have a left hand.' Many of these people are constituents who have seen me in public and on video. I am proud to know that my fellow citizens look upon me in the same manner that I consider myself. My friends do not and have never considered me 'physically challenged.' " [82]

"There are, and always will always be, slight differences. I hug with one arm. I dance with one arm. I hold my wife, Maggie, and my son, Kenny with one arm. However, for all these pleasures, I find that two arms are not necessary." [83]

"Society and our communities in general, have too many physical barriers. It is true that in most cases, these barriers were never intended to place in jeopardy the physically challenged. Some of the obvious obstacles are multistoried buildings with no elevators, which would make it virtually impossible for anyone who had lost the use of his lower extremities to get to a floor above the ground. However, things are much, much better since the passage of the American Disabilities Act." [84]

Inouye advises young people with or without a physical challenge, who would like to pursue a career in politics: "First, study the lives of one or two contemporary politicians and look into their daily lives, personal and public, in some depth. The life of a politician is very difficult for most to follow. [He] must be prepared to live in a 'glass fishbowl.' He must be willing to forego the acquisition of personal riches, must be 'cleaner than a hound's tooth,' and must not do anything to excess, whether it be eating, drinking or having fun.

"You must be careful how you dress, how you present yourself in public. However, having set forth the above, I can say that the life of a politician, because of the many challenges, has psychic rewards. I would recommend a career in politics for those who find that they have an overwhelming desire to serve their fellow man. It is not only noble and honorable, it can be personally very satisfying." [85]

In April 1962, Oren E. Long, the Democratic Senator for Hawaii, told Inouye that he was not going to run again and hoped the younger man would run in his place. A week later Inouye announced his candidacy. His opponent was Ben Dillingham, son of the wealthiest man in the islands, a well-known descendant of generations of conservative Republicans. [86]

Inouye had to spend most of his time on the job in Washington while Maggie campaigned for him. She did well and when her husband finally got home in October, Dillingham challenged him to a debate. The topic was foreign affairs. It was just after the Cuban missile crisis. During the debate, Dillingham made the disastrous mistake of accusing President Kennedy of using this as a "political gimmick" to get more votes. Inouye rebuked him on the platform and from then on, steadily gained ground. By 8 p.m. on election night, Inouye had a two to one lead. Dillingham conceded at 10 p.m. [87]

Inouye reflected at this point: "I was going to the Senate...to the very highest reaches of my government, I, Dan Inouye, who had been raised in respectable poverty and whose father had been born in a tiny Japanese fishing village....I was not of the western world. But fact is that there was really not so great a difference between my story and the stories of millions of other Americans who had come to this land from Ireland and Italy and Poland and Greece. They had come because America would permit any man to aspire to the topmost limits of his talent and energy. I am proud to be one with those people." [88]

Inouye was especially proud that his father, who had been unable to come to his swearing in at the House of Representatives because of a heart attack, was to be a guest of honor at the senatorial ceremony. "In a certain sense, January 9, 1963, belonged to him." [89]

After the ceremony, the Majority Leader, Mike Mansfield, invited Daniel, his father and two brothers to lunch in his private dining room. In the middle of lunch the phone rang. President John F. Kennedy suggested they all come to the White House the following morning. The President took them on a personal tour of the White House and his photo was taken with the new Senator and his father.

As the family left, the press besieged them, and Inouye turned the occasion over to his father. When the media finally quieted down, the elder Inouye said, quietly but with enormous dignity: "I want to thank the people of Hawaii for their goodness to my son, for sending him to the Senate. For me, for myself, I have seen my son become a Senator. I have been invited to eat lunch with the Majority Leader of the Senate and now I have met the President of the United States. Nothing that happens to me now can be greater. I will die a happy man." [90]

A photo of Hyotaro Inouye and John F. Kennedy hangs on the

wall of the house on Coyne Street. The Inouye tradition continued when, on July 14, 1964, Daniel and Maggie's first child, a son, was born six times the eldest son of an eldest son. He was named Daniel Ken Jr. [91] Soon after this, Inouye wrote his autobiography, *Journey to Washington*, because: "It suddenly seemed important that I remember for my son every way station along the roads that had led to his appearance on earth." [92]

In the years that followed Inouye reaped a new harvest of honors. In 1968 he delivered the keynote address at the Democratic National Convention. In 1973, he gained national recognition as a member of the Senate Watergate Committee. In 1979, he became Secretary of the Democratic Conference and continued in this post until 1984 when he chaired the Senate Democratic Central America Study Group to assess U.S. policy, and served as Senior Counselor to the National Bipartisan Commission on Central America, also known as the "Kissinger Commission." In 1987, he became Chairman of the Senate Select Committee on Secret Military Assistance to Iran and the Nicaraguan Opposition, which held public hearings on Iran-Contra from May through August 1987. In 1991, he became Chairman of the Democratic Steering Committee and from 1989 until 1994 he was Chairman of the Committee on Indian Affairs. [93]

Senator Inouye has also served in the following leadership positions: Chairman of the Select Committee on Indian Affairs, which looks into issues affecting Native Hawaiians; Chairman of the Senate Appropriations Subcommittee on Defense; Chairman of the Senate Commerce, Science and Transportation Subcommittee on Communications. [94]

In 1997 "Time-Life Books" chose to honor Inouye in a limited gallery of WW II heroes, which also included George Bush, Joe DiMaggio, Joe Louis, John F. Kennedy, Clark Gable and Jimmy Stewart.

After 40 years of continuous service in Congress, 37 in the Senate, Daniel K. Inouye began his seventh term as Senator in January 1999. He was then the third highest ranking Democrat.

Perhaps the best estimate of Senator Inouye's accomplishments came from Mike Mansfield, the man who invited him to lunch the day he entered the Senate. It was written as a foreword to *Journey to Washington*, but remains a compelling summary of a remarkable life: "It is the story of the Oriental migration, and particularly of Japanese migration—from its painful beginning to its permanent rooting in the United States....The life of Dan Inouye has carried him from the streets of Honolulu into war, into law and into political leadership in Hawaii and...into the Senate of the United States as the first American senator of Japanese ancestry. Dan Inouye's life is a personal triumph, a triumph of a man's courage and determination. But his triumph is, in the end, the triumph of America. The recognition which has come to Dan Inouye, like others before him, reveals the resilient capacity of this nation for replenishment, with energy and wisdom drawn from the many well-springs of the human race. The story of Daniel Ken Inouye, American, is, in truth, an enduring chapter in the story of America." [95]

The quotations in this chapter taken from Senator Daniel Inouye's book, *Journey to Washington*, are reprinted with the permission of Simon & Schuster from *Journey to Washington* by Senator Daniel K. Inouye with Lawrence Elliott. Copyright © by Prentice-Hall, Inc., renewed 1995 by Senator Daniel K. Inouye.

See end notes

# "DISABLED DOES NOT MEAN UNABLE"

## Nancy Rae Litteral

Nancy Rae working at home

## "DISABLED DOES NOT MEAN UNABLE"

## Nancy Rae Litteral

"I paint every day except Sunday. One must have discipline and a schedule. It's my career," says Nancy Rae Litteral as she patiently works on a portrait of a child in her sunny studio. A quadriplegic for 42 years, and today a nationally and internationally known painter, she creates between 30 and 40 paintings a year, runs a one-woman show of her own art work annually, and makes time to help and encourage others who are physically challenged. She is a wise, tolerant, humorous and talented person.

It has not always been like this. From the time of her accident in 1954 to her present success has been a long, hard road. "I did not deal with it at all well at first," she is frank to admit. "I cried most of the time and said 'Why me?' I felt God was unfair and felt sorry for myself. I prayed to die if I could not be healed."

Nancy Rae, who lives with her parents in Wheelersburg, Ohio, was 17 years old in the spring of 1954. She was a member of her high school singing sextet which had won second place on a national TV show in New

York City. She was looking forward to graduation and then college, like the rest of her classmates. Her suitcases for the trip to college were already bought.

"May 4th was a lovely warm day," she recalls. "The Sextet was singing during the Senior Class play intermission. Our car was in the garage for repairs so I walked to school that night. After the play, friends offered me a ride home. On the way home we were hit head-on by a car with five kids in it who had been drinking. The next thing I knew I was lying on the floor without any movement or feeling."

In the hospital the doctors set her broken neck but gave her family no encouragement, since few people with such severe injuries live more than a few days. Her parents took turns sleeping at the hospital. One night she asked her father to read her the 23rd Psalm. When he finished she asked him: "Daddy, if I die, will I see you in heaven?" He left the room without answering and Nancy Rae asked one of the nurses to call the family pastor. That night, her father, who was the only member of the family who had left the church some years before, rejoined and "re-dedicated his life to the Lord."

"Even though the doctors hadn't expected me to live I started to get stronger...our prayers were answered." However, her family members were told that she would almost certainly be paralyzed for life from the neck down. At first she thought it would just be a matter of time before she could walk again; she expected to put off college for a year. After nine weeks in the hospital, several of the doctors said they could do nothing more and sent her home. Then began "the worst year of my life."

In the meantime, the rest of her class had graduated and her chair, left empty, had roses placed in it for the occasion. She was given her diploma. A healthy, vigorous young woman, full of hopes for the future--she planned to be a teacher or a nurse--was suddenly alone, cut off from her friends, "looked after like a baby. I was depressed, full of self-pity and felt my life had ended."

If former classmates came to the house to visit her, to show her photos of college or their later weddings, "I kept a good front while they were there and then cried my eyes out by myself, I was missing out on life, I thought God hadn't answered our prayers, didn't know or care."

This way of life improved somewhat when, in 1955, the doctors suggested Miss Litteral go to Ohio State University for therapy. For the first time she was put in a wheelchair, "which gave me mobility and made life more bearable." She was taught to type with a stick in her teeth and to hold a pen and write with her right hand which still had some movement. Most important, she met other young quadriplegics, some worse than herself; they all encouraged each other and "learned to laugh again."

When Nancy Rae left Ohio State she was advised to "find something to do." She gradually realized that she "still had my eyes and ears and mind," and began to come to terms with her handicap. She and her sister and brothers had been brought up in a local Baptist Church and all had a strong religious faith. At this crucial period in her life, Nancy Rae discovered untapped reserves of healing power. Two passages from the scriptures touched deep chords: "And we know that all things work together for good to them who love God, to them that are called according to his purpose..." (Romans 8:28) and "I can do all things through Christ who strengtheneth me." (Phil. 4:13). Beliefs established in childhood came to her rescue when most needed.

If Nancy Rae found inspiration in the written words in the scriptures, she found living examples of Christian goodness in the attitude of both her parents who looked after her: "they are the most sacrificing parents I know," she says. "They accepted the situation as God's will and looked after me not grudgingly but with love...they gave up vacations, travel, things they wanted to do as they grew older. My mother is 85, my father was 89 when he died on Christmas Eve, 1998. They have both been heroic. We spent every day together."

The whole family was a great support. One brother, David, went into the grocery business with Nancy's father. Another brother, Robert and his wife, Shirley, are missionaries in New Guinea and have brought up three children "in the field." Her sister, Anna Lou, was Nancy's best friend for many years. When Anna Lou's husband was sent to Vietnam in the late '60s, she and her children came to live near her parents and Nancy Rae for a time.

In occupational therapy at Ohio State Nancy had learned to "paint by numbers" as a way of passing the time. Eventually, despite the fact that in school she did not like art at all, she found she wanted to do something on her own artistically, and took a correspondence course in art, beginning in 1960.

She stuck to this for three years and at last began to sell her paintings. "This was a great thrill."

A daily routine was established, that is still, after several decades, Nancy Rae's regular schedule. For 40 years, her mother got her up, gave her breakfast, bathed her, and helped her get to her wheelchair. Recently, due to her parent's failing health, this responsibility has been taken over by a nursing assistant. Nancy Rae uses a lift to get in and out of the wheelchair. In the afternoon she paints for four hours or more and until he died her father cleaned up the paint. She rests after supper, then reads, does her own accounts, writes her own checks. Sometimes she watches a little TV. After evening prayers she goes to bed at 11 p.m. This routine varies only on Sunday when the family goes to church.

Religion has played a major role in Nancy Rae's life. She credits God with any success she has had as a painter and sends most of her profits to help missions and missionary work. She remembers that "as a child, growing up, there were often missionaries in the house, visiting from all over the world. I got used to this. Today we need a worldwide view of spreading the gospel. And the Bible must be translated into many foreign languages."

The combination of her artistic success and her religious faith gradually brought Nancy Rae to a greater acceptance of her situation and the idea that "trials and tribulations are a preparation for heaven, and make you more aware of the needs of others."

When she was living in Wheelersburg, Anna Lou, her sister, showed Nancy a verse from Thessalonians, 5:8 which urges that one should: "In everything give thanks, for this is the will of God in Christ Jesus concerning you." This verse enabled Nancy to take a new outlook and actually brought her "real joy."

The family's strong faith was severely tested in April 1968, when Anna Lou was caught in a tornado that struck her brother's house and died three days later. She left three young boys to be brought up by others.

The death of this beloved sister and her first year as a quadriplegic were undoubtedly the low points of Nancy's whole life. The highest point, which she remembers with pride, was when, after many years of effort, she was finally accepted as a member of the Association of Mouth and Foot Painting Artists, a branch of the Association of Handicapped Artists.

This prestigious organization is hard to join. It has publishing houses all over the world, and is unusual because each office in each country is run by handicapped people of that country; few organizations are run that way. Nancy Rae is one of 200 people with a full international membership. Full members and others, numbering approximately 1,000, are on scholarship, and receive a monthly stipend. Each month, all sales internationally are totaled and expenses taken out. Then the remaining monies are divided among members, which enables them to pursue their careers without financial worries and provides for trips and visits to exhibits (Nancy Rae was invited to a conference in Vienna in May 1997).

The monthly amount each person receives varies, depending on general sales, but at the end of each year every individual member gets a bonus on any of their own paintings that were published in cards, calendars or notes. Nancy Rae submits about ten paintings a year and is remunerated according to how many are chosen by the judging panel of artists.

Doctor Richard Hope, Art Historian, said in one of his articles about AMFPA: "The Association of Mouth and Foot Painting Artists (AMFPA) counts among the most consistent models of cultural self-help in this day and age....AMFPA artists gain equal status with their fellow citizens as active members of society. They can organize their lives, support their families, and find self-fulfillment in their art....for the artists themselves and for the general public, the feeling of self-esteem gained from their cultural activities is equally essential. The AFMPA strengthens this feeling through publications, film documentation, lectures, exhibits and public relations work. Contacts among artists, between their galleries and publishing companies, are encouraged at conventions and artists' meetings.

The Association has been especially helpful to Nancy's career by helping to promote her greeting cards in many parts of the United States and the rest of the world. Christmas cards are a large part of the Association's overall business, and Nancy Rae is also one of a group whose paintings are reproduced for use in calendars.

Nancy Rae also accepts private commissions. She has become better known since she started having "an art show once a year in which I enter my paintings in the County Fair. People hear about me through word of mouth and come to the house. They bring photographs of what they want painted. I've painted helicopters, boats, cars, dogs and cats, and, of course, portraits of loved ones."

Nancy Rae's favorite subject continues to be children and she has become keenly aware how much she regrets not having a child of her own. "What I miss most is to take a child in my arms."

Her determination to succeed as a painter was severely tested when, after "years of using my right elbow too much, arthritis set in, making it impossible for me to use my right arm." So she started painting by mouth, encouraged by the example of Joni Eraeckson Tada, who had always had to paint in this way. A dentist made her a special apparatus to protect her teeth so she can paint for hours at a time. "I do some watercolors but mostly use oil paints, painting landscapes, still lifes, portraits, just about any subject."

Her technique is unusual and exacting. Since she sketches by mouth, a precise plan is required for every painting. Because she does not create a painting from a blank canvas, but needs something to look at--a photograph of a horse, a barn, a fruit or something else--she has a copy made of a photograph, preferably an 8x10 studio photograph, then blocks it off in one-inch squares, using these to code it up to sketch onto to a larger canvas. Patiently, with the brush in her teeth, she tackles one square at a time. Because of this complicated planning, she considers herself "a painter, not an artist."

Her paint brushes have magnetic handles so she can change them at will without having to ask her mother for help. "People of varying ages-- especially children--are the most difficult to do but, at the same time, are the most satisfying." Working at least four hours every afternoon, she completes a typical portrait in "from 10 days to two weeks."

Nancy Rae uses humor in dealing with her own disability, saying "you have to laugh at yourself [in order] not to cry." And laughter can help her deal better with the attitude of others to her condition.

"Children are instinctively curious. I don't mind answering their questions. Older people will feel spontaneous sympathy and pat me on the head saying, 'Aw, honey.' This I can handle because it is real and natural. What gets to me is those who 'Gawk' in restaurants. Once I went out to eat with my parents and two women at the next table stared at me all through the meal. I didn't go back to a restaurant for a longtime."

She constantly reaches out to help others: ''Help for physically challenged and disabled people must be not only in architectural structures and general technology but in peoples' minds and hearts," she said. She feels that conditions have been greatly improved recently. "Forty five years ago it was hard...the bank still had two steps...I had trouble getting into the Ohio State University Library, even with the help of friends. Now I can go to the bank or the store. And there is more recovery now. Shots given right after accidents can prevent this sort of paralysis."

Her greatest fear today is getting a cold or the flu or a similar illness. She cannot cough on her own and phlegm accumulates. If she is ill she has to be hospitalized. "This is scary," she admits, "Joni [Eraeckson Tada] and I have this in common. We can't lie down to sleep at night if we have a cold."

Nancy Rae admires what people can now do athletically despite disabilities. "More has been done recently to help them--braces, racing wheelchairs, marathon races for wheelchairs--technology has come a long way. These people have to learn to adjust their bodies like astronauts in space."

Her advice to the newly injured and disabled: "Don't sit and watch TV all day. Get an interest--a hobby--and follow it! Take a correspondence course. Learn to use a computer. Follow through!"

Nancy Rae is particularly sympathetic to children and young people who have faced such challenges from birth. "I had 18 years of running and playing. They never had that. They need a friend, someone to smile at them...that can make their day--you should get down on their level. People tower over those in wheelchairs, which can be frightening."

She is very aware of the problems of others. "I'm fairly well-known now and get more attention, therefore. People will say: 'Nancy Rae--she paints--I know her.' Others need more help."

AMFPA celebrated its 40th anniversary in the spring of 1998. As part of this, Nancy was flown to Vienna where her Easter Calendar with a painting of her grand-niece holding a basket of eggs, was displayed for a month in the Vienna City Hall.

What counsel can she give to young people who are worried about peer pressure, sex appeal, good looks, athletics, drugs, popularity? This wise and courageous woman has a simple message: "We are all valuable. When something happens to you, as it did to me, you realize all those things are not important at all.

"You won't always be young and beautiful. It's what's inside that makes a person beautiful. But you have one earthly body and you should take care of it, not abuse it with drugs and alcohol. Take good care of it-- it's the only one you've got. Be thankful for it."

Thankfulness for what she can still do is a running theme in Nancy Rae Litteral's life. "<u>Disabled</u> does not mean <u>unable</u>," she says firmly. We must not dwell on the things we cannot do, but focus on the many things we can still do...Painting gives me something to look forward to each day, a challenge.

"I thank God for the ability I have. Whatever circumstances you are in, you can live a happy, joyful life. God has been good to me and blessed me with a wonderful, supportive family, friends and church. I couldn't have made it without God's love or their help.  God bless you all."

## "KID, YOU'VE GOT IT!"

### Ken "Muck" Meyer, Interviewer Extraordinaire

# "KID, YOU'VE GOT IT!"

## Ken "Muck" Meyer, Interviewer Extraordinaire

*Ken "Muck" Meyer, currently on the Commissioner's staff for Persons with Disabilities in Boston, Massachusetts, is better known as a former radio personality for WBZ and WEEI and host of WEEI's Old-Time Radio programs, called Radio Classics.*

Ken Meyer is an avid Boston Red Sox fan, but he's never seen the emerald green grass of the outfield at Fenway Park, the crisp, white home flannel uniforms with their red piping and lettering trimmed in black, or the dark green left field wall known around the world as the "Green Monster." Even though he has been to Fenway Park many times both for professional and personal reasons, Ken Meyer has never seen these things--but millions of radio listeners have heard him describe them.

Ken Meyer has been blind from birth, but this challenge has not prevented his pursuing a career in broadcast journalism and, more recently, as an advocate for the disabled in the City of Boston.

"When I was a kid I watched baseball games on the radio," he recalls. "On Saturday nights, I used to ride around in the car with my Dad, and listen to ball games from Yankee Stadium. Mickey Mantle was my hero, and I heard Roger Maris hit his 61st home run. There was no bigger thrill...those were great days."

"Rochester, where I grew up, was the home of the farm club for the St. Louis Cardinals. Tom Decker, who is now with the National Safety Council in Chicago, used to broadcast the games for Rochester. One of the great rivalries in the International League was between Rochester and Buffalo. Bill Mazur, who now works in television in New York City, used to call the games for Buffalo. I could get both stations, so I'd switch back and forth between them."

Meyer's early fascination with radio and sports carried over into most of his professional life. His ears became his eyes in a very real sense. He firmly believes that radio was good for youngsters because it required them to use their imaginations.

"You have to create the characters of radio plays yourself," he said. "Take the character of Matt Dillon in the program 'Gunsmoke.' The radio actor, William Conrad, had a great, deep voice which made you imagine a big, tall man. When the series went on TV, they had to replace Conrad with James Arness, because Conrad was a short, fat guy. Arness did not have the voice or the acting ability but he looked the way people imagined Matt Dillon should look."

"In front of the radio anybody is sightless. The actors create for you and you imagine the rest. My mother used to record soap operas for me when I was in school. I lived for sports and those other programs."

Meyer's love for baseball was heightened by a high school camping trip in a trailer with other students. The gym teacher took a group to the Baseball Hall of Fame in Cooperstown, New York. Young Ken knew that the director of this organization who met them there had written for the Times-Mirror newspaper chain, and made an immediate hit by mentioning this. As a result, the director opened the cases and made sure that Ken "had the first chance at handling the things in the cases...the hat that Koufax wore...the uniform that Babe Ruth wore...it was a great thrill."

Meyer took his share of lumps growing up in Rochester. Although he played with other neighborhood kids: "They would forget and leave bikes in the middle of the road. I would be running along and go head over heels. But we'd still roller skate together."

Young Ken attended the State School for the Blind in Batavia where all students had a vision impairment of one sort or another. "Our school competed with other schools in athletics, track, and so on. The orchestra and the chorus went to other schools with sighted kids."

College, however, was a different matter. "There I was the exception and not the rule," he observed. "In school I took notes with a braille machine; in college the teachers said it made too much noise. I had to tape classes, get notes from other kids or just remember. As a result I did not care for Western Civilization, English, or history courses. So I took a course in broadcasting."

In Boston, Meyer had the good fortune to meet Dick Walsh, the Director of Engineering at Graham Junior College. "Dick was a great mentor of mine," he said. "One of my heroes besides Mel Allen was Phil Rizzuto. I asked Dick if he could arrange for me to interview Rizzuto sometime when he was in town and he did.

"I can remember the date. It was May 19, 1968, a Sunday afternoon. I sat in a room under the stands at Fenway Park and interviewed Rizzuto for half an hour. Walsh heard the tape the next day. After it was over, he shook my hand. You could feel him shaking, he was so excited. He said: 'Kid, you've got it. Maintain that style and you're going to be one of the best successes in broadcasting.' His saying that brought tears to my eyes."

Meyer made a documentary about Rizzuto later, during his senior year in college, complete with script, narration, and music, for which he received an "A".

"The '50s and '60s were made for sports...I loved that era...When I came to Boston I was in my early 20s and it was just before the Red Sox won the pennant in 1967," Meyer says. He tried to break into broadcasting and was asked such discouraging questions as: "Gee, how can I give you a job? You haven't got any experience."

In 1971, Ken got his first break from Bill Schubert, doing an evening show on WBZ: "Schubert had a son who was deaf and I think he thought if he helped me, someone might give his son a break," said Meyer.

Meyer took his break and ran with it, and by 1972, he was producing the radio show "Calling All Sports" hosted by John Carlson. "There I was, not having been at the station for a year, doing a program from 8 p.m. to midnight. Then one day when John Carlson was on the road and everybody else was out of town for one reason or another, I hosted the show. I was scared silly.

My mother and father were listening on the car radio in Rochester and they were as nervous as I was. My dad nearly drove off the road when he heard me blow a line."

Meyer admits that what made him nervous was the realization that "people in 38 states are hearing this!" He finally came to terms with his emotions by broadcasting on "a one-to-one basis...just you and the personality...from then on, it was a breeze..."

John Carlson says, "Ken was the WBZ veteran and I was the rookie, riding a wheezing steed up from Brockton to challenge the Boston windmill. We shared our visions of radio and our hopes for a place in the medium. We shared, too, our gratitude for the chance in Boston and the determination to do something with the opportunity. Ken has graced the memory of that opportunity with his success but, best of all, he remains my friend."

"Guy Manilla was a big deal then," says Meyer. "I still have tapes of him with Bobby Orr. Nobody could write like Manilla. Nobody can now and this is still missing from sports broadcasting today."

Meyer began to make an impression on the WBZ pundits when he persuaded celebrities like Carl Yastrzemski and Joe Namath to grant lengthy interviews. "They thought 'he can get anybody' and began asking me to do things that were just impossible.' "

In 1972 he started filling in on the Larry Glick show. In this situation he soon realized "I had to be myself...I couldn't be Larry Glick...from then on it was a ball. It's almost 25 years later and I still get excited thinking about those interviews." It was Glick who gave him his nickname "Muck" from a radio show that was popular in the '70s, "Muck and Mire."

"One night on my show, I was talking by phone to some crazy kid who wanted to be in radio," Glick said later. "I had him do a station promo on the air and made my pronouncement: 'Kid,' I said, 'give it up. You'll never make it.' As fate would have it, this same kid actually became my producer--the best in the business."

In what he considers his "golden years" Meyer interviewed Lowell Thomas, Howard K. Smith and Bob Hope as well as Mel Blanc--"the Man of a Thousand Voices," during the 50th Anniversary year of WBZ. In 1974 he was involved in a three-hour tribute to Jack Benny. "I met a lot of stars. My sightlessness helped in a lot of the interviews, because, since I had never mentioned my disability to the stars, they told me more stuff than they told other people..."

Larry Glick says, "Muck possesses the incredible gift of refusing to believe in the words 'it can't be done.' " His determination, his tenacity, is incredible. Who else could have tracked down Johnny Cash in Israel just because I wanted to interview him on my midnight to dawn show?"

Meyer took his preparation seriously. If a star had written a book, he made a point of calling the publisher ahead of time and getting a synopsis, "so I wouldn't look stupid." His interviewees were impressed with his research.

"Research pays off," he says. "I can't stand those who do an interview without first reading the book. The author has a certain view he wants to convey to his audience and you have to read the book so you can convey this. You can't just glance at the book jacket and expect to get away with it." (Meyer has a particular dislike for Larry King's present-day style.) Meyer's system worked. The Lennon sisters were so impressed with him they told him it was "the best interview we've ever had..."

Asked if he was nervous when he first began interviewing, Meyer responds: "Yes, especially if it was somebody I worshipped, like Curt Gowdy. I was so nervous I wrote out a whole bunch of notes ahead of time. But after the second question I took the notes and threw them on the floor. I always wanted to look my best...preparation is the big thing."

There was a memorable time when Meyer was caught unprepared.

Gowdy had arranged for him to interview the formidable Howard Cosell. This he did over lunch at the Marriott Hotel. Cosell barked at him: "TURN ON YOUR TAPE RECORDER AND LET'S GO!" When Meyer got back to WBZ afterwards he discovered that he had "the most beautiful piece of blank tape I've ever had in my life!"

Luckily Gowdy was able to arrange a second interview--one that was only fifteen minutes long. "Cosell did not complain. It turned out he had the same experience when he was young with Sandy Koufax. Maybe that was one reason he was nice to me..." Meyer's opinion is that Cosell's bark was worse than his bite. "A lot of it was bluster..."

Asked about the low points in his life, Meyer replies: "When I was out of work. I had left WBZ for WEEI and then was let go. I was doing temporary work and was in the depths of depression. I had visions of going bankrupt.

"Soon after that I was invited back to WEEI to broadcast. They phoned and asked me if I was interested. I had the good sense to say: 'Perhaps, if equitable financial arrangements can be worked out,' instead of shouting 'YES!'"

"They took me to breakfast and treated me like a king. The whole thing took about five minutes to work out but the man hiring me wanted 'to stay down here a little longer so the Manager will think we've had a hard time.'" Meyer started back at WEEI November 1988.

Meyer went on to interview Steve Allen, Dick Clark and Bob Hope as well as Mickey Mantle in Yankee Stadium. He treasures a photo taken of him with Mantle by a passing photographer.

Ken also recalls with pride his friendship with former Boston Bruins coach Don Cherry. "Don Cherry used to play and coach in my home town of Rochester. I covered every game he coached. I interviewed him when his book came out. Cherry was a decent human being."

Meyer became more aware of disabled people when he helped raise funds for Cotting School in 1989. He was then at WEEI and agreed to help a friend, Kelly Clark, raise money for the school with the proviso: "that I enjoyed my work, did it well, and was willing to help--not that I could not see. That's how I got involved with Cotting School," says Meyer.

Cotting School made Meyer more sensitive to other disabled people. Is it better to be born blind? "There are arguments both ways," Meyer replies. "It may help in some areas, but not in others. You don't have to worry about adjusting later in life.

"I often wonder what would have happened if I had been able to see for nine or ten years. I would know about color. I would be able to travel better. There are advantages and disadvantages both ways. You can't miss something you've never had.

"The new ADA laws have helped the disabled to an extent, but there will always be prejudice against someone with a disability. In a restaurant someone will ask my companion: 'Does he want anything else?' and I say 'Why don't you ask <u>me</u>?' In his present capacity as staff member of the Commission for Persons with Disabilities at Boston City Hall, Meyer has been able to campaign for braille on the elevator in his own condo building, for taxis that can handle wheelchairs and in various other areas.

He has been in this job since 1989 and has seen a lot of discrimination. What can he do? "I can call people about laws they are unaware of. For instance, you can't discriminate against someone because they have a guide dog."

Although he feels discrimination will always exist, Meyer believes... "there are some good-hearted people out there and the good outweighs the bad. All in all, Boston and Massachusetts are ahead of other places in their dealings with the disabled.

"The main thing society needs to do for the disabled is to treat people like human beings...don't talk down to them or at them, talk with them.!"

Meyer advises those with a disability to act like ordinary people and not to feel too sorry for themselves. They, after all, have a responsibility too. "If you don't get up in the morning and show up for work you'll get canned as quickly as anyone else."

With his own record of long years of hard work, Meyer is not afraid to make this point loud and clear.

He feels that computers are playing a big role in helping the disabled. He wonders "what the world will be like in five years...I won't be surprised if they have a car rigged up so a computer can drive it. Man, I just can't get that out of my mind. Wouldn't I love to be in a car driving around with the windows down and listening to a ball game."

Part of Meyer's responsibility is to counsel elderly people who are losing their sight. He urges them to accept "talking books," and recordings. "Sometimes they'll accept them, sometimes they won't." Meyer himself doesn't have that worry. He's been reading with his ears since boyhood and knows more about most sports than those of us who can see.

He'll go on "watching" ball games and hockey as he has always done, and telling the rest of us about the high points.

# "SPIRIT IN THE DARK"

## Diane Schuur

Diane with "Socks", President Clinton's cat

Diane with husband "Rocket"

## "SPIRIT IN THE DARK"

## Diane Schuur

*"I couldn't believe what I heard. This girl had the range of somebody with depth and staying power. She takes from the tradition of an Ella and a Sarah and what comes out is her own achievement of that tradition."*

Stan Getz
Monterey Jazz Festival, 1981

"This month I rode a horse for the first time in years," Diane Schuur said enthusiastically in mid-January 1997. The blind jazz singer had just returned from a holiday in Hawaii, where she celebrated the first anniversary of her marriage to retired aerospace executive, Les Crockett, on January 13, 1996.

The two met on a Holland American jazz cruise in October 1995. In the words of one of the cuts in her recent album: "Love Walked In," suddenly and unexpectedly.

In her professional life, Diane has inspired raves from around the

*"Blessed with a clear, ringing voice, Schuur has emerged as the singer most likely to carry on the pop tradition of Ella Fitzgerald."*
*--The New York Times.*

world as the "new first lady of jazz." She has twice played the White House, and her recordings continue to top the charts. She

119

has been nominated five times for Grammy awards, winning in 1986 for her album "Timeless" and again, in 1988, for "Diane Schuur and the Count Basie Orchestra."

Schuur is a top jazz singer whose star is still rising. After hearing her sing at the Monterey Jazz Festival more than 18 years ago, the late jazz saxophonist, Stan Getz, said of her talent: "She's got an incredible range...she can sing almost any style from scat to country ballads that can tear your heart out...in my opinion, Diane's got all the equipment to be one of the greats. She is the logical successor to Ella [Fitzgerald] and Sarah [Vaughn]."

*"For years I thought Barbra Streisand was the best singer we had. I think Diane is the best singer we have. Her name is mentioned frequently with those revered matriarchs like Ella Fitzgerald for her phrasing and Dinah Washington for her clarity and quality."--USA Today.*

This 'rave review' was given after hearing Diane "wow the audience with 'Amazing Grace'." Getz remained friend and mentor to Diane right up until his death. The American music loving public has come to agree with Getz's estimate of her singing abilities. Since the early 1980s her career has been a triumph, a life, indeed, "like a song."

The early years were more of a struggle. Diane was born two months prematurely in Tacoma, Washington. She was placed in an incubator and excessive oxygen damaged her optic nerve for life. She has been blind from birth. (Diane's twin brother, David, survived without loss of sight and is now a Federal Aviation Administration inspector and a pilot in his own right.) In contrast, Diane's life has been an uphill fight all the way, but it is a fight she is winning.

*"Amazing vocal versatility and powerful assuredness...her status among her peers is unquestioned."--Tower Pulse.*

"As a very young kid, about two or three, I used to listen to the radio and hear Dinah Washington. I admired her and wanted to emulate her voice, so I shut myself up in a closet about midnight, and started singing. My parents thought I should be asleep and told me to shut up!" Nonetheless, her parents, David and Joan, encouraged their daughter. She was sent to the School for the Blind in Vancouver from age four to eleven

*"I was blown away." Larry Rosen, Producer, GRP Records.*

and came home only on weekends. "I tried singing in school, but some of the kids made fun of me because my voice was so grown up." This did not discourage her. She attended the University in Puget Sound for six months where she was taught operatic techniques "how to breathe through the rib cage, not the throat." This early training helped her in later life. She soon found that her voice was "a bridge to the world."

Diane's mother died when Diane was only 13 and from that point on her father, a police captain, single-handedly brought up Diane, her twin brother and a sister. Diane attended public school in Auburn for several years as a teenager. "This was quite an adjustment."

Diane's career as a singer, however, was already launched. At the age of ten, her mother had taken her to the Holiday Inn in Fife, a suburb of Tacoma, where, although she forgot the words to the song in mid-performance, Diane's voice attracted favorable attention. She sang regularly from that time on. "My first small gigs were 'The Gay '90s' in Moose and Elks Lodges," she recalls, "and by age 14, I was at Lake Tahoe." Unfortunately, her father, whose police work was demanding, could not accompany his daughter on as many concert tours as she might

121

have been offered at this young age.

When she graduated from high school in 1973, Diane began working regularly in top Northwest jazz night clubs. She also learned to read extensively in braille "which widened my imagination and helped me

*"Each era has certain female jazz singers who stand head and shoulders above the rest. For my money, as regards the '80s and '90s, this can be said of Diane Schuur."--The Jazz Rag, Orpington, Kent, Great Britain.*

see how other people lived." She particularly enjoyed reading biographies, such as the stories of

Charlie Parker and Billie Holiday. "I read sometimes until my fingers were raw."

In late 1973, Diane had the chance to audition for the Tonight Show. This did not work out, but as a result of her meeting with the show's drummer, Ed Shaugnessey, Diane was given the opportunity to perform at

*"Aorca Center could not have hoped for a better headliner for its first international jazz and blues festival than American singer, Diane Schuur...there was nothing to really ignite the audience at a packed NZI Convention Hall until Schuur was led on stage...the voice is superb and Schuur shows she is the classic jazz singer of our age...the audience wouldn't let her go."-- The New Zealand Herald , 1993.*

the Monterey Jazz Festival two years later, in 1975.

Diane's battles have not all been for acceptance as a singer in a highly competitive profession. When she spent a few years in Arizona in the

early 1970s, "I got in with the wrong set of people and began to drink heavily. I was discouraged at that time." Despite her discouragement she kept on singing, but "bills piled up and eventually I was forced to go bankrupt." This was, by her own admission, the lowest point in her life.

Diane fought alcoholism for years and she did not give up. At her second visit to the Monterey Jazz Festival in 1981, Stan Getz heard her and "wanted to make me a star." This fortuitous meeting led to a performance

122

in the White House in 1982, along with other stars. This was during the Reagan Administration and Diane was "electrifying." Nancy Reagan

*"If you're talking Judy Garland on a good day...you could listen to Diane Schuur...her voice is pure silver. She scats and soars with such ease...although there are some elements of her style which seem to derive from her great predecessors, she nonetheless maintains a strong individual identity..."--The Singer, Kent, Great Britain, 1996.*

remains one of her fans, as was Frank Sinatra. (When she stayed in the Sinatras' West Coast home, after a benefit performance for one of Mrs Sinatra's favorite charities, Frank told Diane that he wished he could give her one of his own eyes.)

Following White House appearances in 1982 and 1984, one triumph succeeded another. Larry Rosen, of GRP Records, who heard her first D.C. performance, was quick to sign her, and she has been recording hits under the GRP label ever since. By 1999 she has completed 13 albums,

*"When Diane Schuur won the 'Best Female Jazz Vocal Performance' Grammy, her competition was Carmen McRae and Ella Fitzgerald."--Associated Press.*

the latest being "Music Is My Life." Her husband's favorite song is "Blue Gardenia" from the album "Love Walked In." This charming song was the soundtrack of "Bridges of Madison County" starring Meryl Streep and Clint Eastwood.

Diane Schuur's career in recent years has been a whirlwind of festivals around the world and concert tours and recording sessions at home. She has performed on every continent--with the exception of Africa--several times in Japan, South America and Great Britain. In 1996 she appeared in Bangkok, Thailand as a part of King Bhumibol Adulayadel's Golden Anniversary Concerts, celebrating the King's 50 years on the throne. In 1997 she performed at the Red Sea Jazz Festival in Israel which was a colossal success, attended by thousands. A few years ago, in connection with the Performance Rights Bill, she met President Clinton and Congressional leaders, and took special delight in being

introduced to the President's cat, "Socks." (Diane is a cat lover.)

Diane, or "Deedles," as she likes to be called, has a buoyant, bouncy personality and a capacity to make everyone else feel like singing too. "When I'm on stage," she says, "I feel like I want to go out in the audience and hug everybody...it's a love exchange." She does not let her lack of sight inhibit her in the slightest. She has appeared regularly on the

Tonight Show in the past decade, and once floored the formidable Johnny Carson by exclaiming: "God, you look handsome tonight!"

Deedles gives a lot of praise to her manager, Paul Cantor, who came into her life in 1984. "My income took an upward leap when he took over," she says joyfully. "Pauly Wauly," as he is nicknamed by his irrepressible client, has become a mainstay in her career. She considers the high points in her professional life, the landmark events of which she is proudest, to be her appearances in Carnegie Hall. The first was in 1988, when she was invited to be part of a tribute to Irving Berlin; in 1993 she was included there in a tribute to Ella Fitzgerald, and in an all-star memorial to the same singer in 1996. She also sang on this New York City stage in the summer of 1997 in an accolade to the late Nat "King" Cole, and, again, in 1998 as part of an all-star tribute to Frank Sinatra.

Deedles still considers herself a recovering alcoholic, but she is on top of the situation now. She urges others not to keep such a problem a secret but to seek help and face the issue openly.

In her leisure time, when she is not on tour, she likes to watch videos with her husband and is renewing an interest in horseback riding. She and her husband, "Rocket," live in a retirement community when they are in California. This community provides horses. The Crocketts also have a home in Bellevue, Washington, Diane's home state, which is referred to as "The Deedle Pad." "Rocket" travels with his wife on her tours. Their marriage seems to be one long romance.

Two of Diane's best friends are the cats, "Sabe" in California (imported from her husband's home in San Jose), and "Weedle" in Washington. "Weedle" is jealous of "Rocket" at present but Deedles anticipates the cat will get over this.

Diane's reaction to what needs to be done by the private and public sectors to help the physically challenged in the 21st century is swift and precise: "It's not mostly a matter of ramps and access, it's much more a question of attitude," she says. "Don't look at us as either above you or beneath you. Look at us as equals, as people, not non-people. Sometimes others will shout at me in a restaurant or elsewhere because they assume I'm deaf as well as blind. This is disconcerting." However, she gives credit to ADA for the existence of braille in elevators, captions in TV programs, and other improvements that have taken place in recent years.

Her advice to those who may become blind in later life and still want to pursue a performing arts career: "Get a good lawyer to represent you before you do anything else. You can get between a rock and a hard place if you can't read a contract. I did. This is very important." Also, she firmly states: "you must believe in yourself and what you want to do. Don't let anyone intimidate you. Have faith in the God of your choice. FOLLOW YOUR DREAM. Don't give up." She continues: "Nothing's going to stop me because the only thing that limits you is your own mind, if you let it. I feel very blessed when I'm on stage."

In 1998, Diane became part of Atlantic Records, a new label. In the same year she was one of only two people ever to be given the Bagley Wright Award for bringing national and international recognition to the city of Seattle. In the same landmark year, while in Hawaii to perform with the Honolulu Symphony, she chose to experience her first sky dive.

This courageous singer, who has fought back against a number of adversities that might have overwhelmed a lesser person, has not only an outstanding talent but a strong and vibrant character, a vigorous enjoyment of life and an ability to bring out the best in other people. She is, most certainly, in the words of one of her songs, a rare and shining "Spirit in the Dark."

Albums: 1980s
"Deedles"
"Schuur Thing"
"Timeless"
"Diane Schuur
  and the Count Basie Orchestra"
"Talkin' 'Bout You"
"Diane Schuur Collection"

Albums: 1990s
"In Tribute (to Dinah Washington)
"Love Songs"
"Heart to Heart"
"Love Walked In"
"Blues for Schuur"
"A Schuur Bet"
"Music is My Life"

# "ONE OF THE LUCKY ONES"

Dr. William Sniger

Dr. William Sniger
Spinal Cord Team
Boston University Hospital

## "ONE OF THE LUCKY ONES"

### Dr. William Sniger

"I'm one of the lucky ones," says Dr. William Sniger as he carefully leaned his crutches against a conference table in the library of the Boston University Hospital of Rehab Medicine. "I'm ambulatory and I can drive a car. I don't consider myself disabled. I am what I am and if people don't like it, tough!"

Dr. Sniger, a quadriplegic since his senior year in high school, is one of only six quadriplegic doctors in the United States. Since 1995 he has been a member of the hospital's Spinal Cord Team. He lives with his parents at his boyhood home in Raynham, Massachusetts and commutes by car to the hospital daily.

In 1971, William Sniger was on the honor roll in high school with plans to attend Harvard and earn a law degree. Those plans were scrapped suddenly when tragedy struck at a summertime pool party.

"I took one more dive before going in, hit my head, and suddenly couldn't move," he recalled. "I knew right away that something was badly wrong because I had first aid training as an Eagle Scout. I held my breath, floated to the surface, and called to my friends for help. They thought at first I was joking."

It quickly became clear that Sniger's condition was no joke. He was rushed to Beth Israel Hospital where it was determined that he had no movement or feeling from the neck down. Instead of going to Harvard that fall, he spent the next 28 months in hospitals. "This was the most depressing time of my life," he said, "getting used to the loss of independence and the ability to do things for oneself, adjusting to the fact that people were staring at me all the time."

When he emerged from the long series of hospital treatments, Sniger worked for the Spinal Cord Society, a national, nonprofit organization with outposts all over the country. He did both fund raising and public relations and became state coordinator for Massachusetts. Although he was not enrolled at Harvard, his keen mind did not go to waste. He admires the Society and still works for it as a volunteer in his "spare" time.

In 1981, William Sniger heard of another quadriplegic who had become a doctor, despite his limitations. He got in touch with this man, and was encouraged to proceed with a similar career if he was so inclined. He decided to pursue this career instead of the law, despite the long periods of college, pre-med and medical school. "I felt it was what I was meant to do," recalled Sniger. He and this doctor are today two of only half a dozen quadriplegic doctors in the United States.

The journey from patient to doctor has been a long and arduous one. After a 12-year forced "sabbatical," he graduated cum laude in his premed courses from the University of Massachusetts in Boston in 1989 and then faced the challenge of finding a medical school that would accept a quadriplegic. He was eventually offered places at Boston University and UMass Worcester. He accepted the latter position and graduated in 1994.

"It's like running a triathlon every day of your life," he says of the process of becoming a physician. "During the four years of medical school plus the additional arduous years of internship and residency training, you're forced to eat, drink and breathe medicine 24 hours a day, seven days a week."

After a year's residency at Brockton Hospital, Dr. Sniger began a three-year residency at Boston University Medical Center where he specialized in spinal cord injuries. The BU Rehab Unit is one of only 18 so designated in America.

"Anyone thinking of pursuing a career in medicine must remember that an average doctor with no handicap works a six-day week with 36-hour shifts, day and night at low pay," he said. "It can be a sacrifice at the best of times. Are you ready for this?

"I, myself work a 100-hour week because it takes me longer to get places--driving, going down corridors, up in elevators and so on." Dr. Sniger uses a scooter to travel long distances up and down the hospital corridors.

Dr. Sniger points out that his own physical condition is an asset because it enables him to establish a better relationship with his patients. "A lot of physicians have difficulty relating to injured patients," he observes, "especially those most recently injured. I see hundreds of people and it is easier for me to establish a good rapport with many of them. I am more fortunate than many because I regained the use of my hands...some have no return of function of any kind."

What can be done to make life easier for the disabled? "The main thing that has to change is people's attitudes," says Sniger. "Marlon Brando's first movie, The Men, is about a paraplegic and states the case very exactly. Brando's character remarks at one point to a man: 'Would you mind if I married your daughter?' and is rebuffed by a blank and dismayed stare. In this movie there are older cars and buildings but remarkably little else has changed. There is still the notion that someone who has limitations cannot have a normal life with a partner...."

Dr. Sniger's advice to the recently disabled is to maintain a positive attitude, stay active and involved, and avoid the 'victim rationale.' "Abolish that philosophy altogether," he says. "It's easy to drift, do nothing and let the years go by. If you drop out, it is very difficult to get back in."

"It's important to identify goals. What did you want to do before? Make plans. Talk to others who have done this. You've only got one life.

It's your decision. Nobody will do it for you."

Dr. Sniger admits that some practical things such as ramps, parking lots and physical set-ups, have changed for the better, but considers the Americans With Disabilities Act (ADA) to be a double-edged sword. "ADA has brought about necessary opportunities for employment, and more tolerance for the physically challenged, but it has also expanded the definition of 'disabled' to include alcoholism and drugs. This means that today, alcoholics and drug addicts compete not only for sympathy, but for housing, parking spaces and employment.

"Nowadays, almost anyone can persuade a doctor to give him or her a handicapped parking sticker. Sometimes I can't find any place open to park myself when I come to work or go elsewhere. Searching for a place can consume a great amount of time...."

Dr. Sniger's use of high technology is limited to a word processor at the moment, but he admits that computers are making life much more comfortable for disabled people who cannot use their hands to turn lights on or off. "Lights can be turned on and off by movements of the mouth, chin or an upper plate worn in the mouth like a denture," he explained. "Also, computers provide electronic stimulation to paralyzed extremities and sometimes restore partial use of hands or limited use of legs not possible before now."

In July, 1998, Dr. Sniger joined the staff of the Veterans Administration Health Care System in New England located in West

Roxbury, Massachusetts. He continues to specialize in working with spinal cord injuries.

Dr. Sniger's long association with the Spinal Cord Society has spurred his own research efforts for a medical cure of spinal cord injuries. "There is no doubt that we have the potential to find a cure for SCI within our lifetime," he predicts. "The problem is funding. SCI is not a priority for the federal government...."

In his leisure time, Dr. Sniger collects classic cars (automobiles more than 25 years old). His family runs a used car business and he is proud of a '66 Oldsmobile and a '70 Pontiac that have been restored to mint condition. He speaks of his cars with the same enthusiasm some people reserve for golf and fishing.

Dr. Sniger's best advice is simple and compelling: "Take one step at a time," he says. "Take that first step, the most difficult of all. A journey of a thousand miles begins with a single pace."

As Dr. William Sniger concluded the discussion and began the long journey back down the corridor to see his next patient, using crutches expertly, one could not help reflecting how much time many of us without disability waste before attempting a similar step on our own life's journey. What is our excuse for delay?

Dr. Sniger is right. He is one of the lucky ones.

# HAPPY TO BE ALIVE

**Darryl Stingley, former New England Patriots football star**

Darryl, All-Pro Wide Receiver

Darryl with friends

# HAPPY TO BE ALIVE

## Darryl Stingley, former New England Patriots football star

If you're a veteran, exhibition games are nothing games in the National Football League; play a quarter or two and then stand on the sidelines while the coaches evaluate the rookies and free agents, and the owners count up the gate receipts.

Darryl Stingley was a veteran. Since graduating from Purdue five years before, he had already reached All-Pro status as one of the most feared wide receivers in the League. He had the courage to run the dangerous, but productive, down and in pattern that frustrated linebackers and defensive backs. He and New England Patriots teammate Stanley Morgan were quarterback Steve Grogan's favorite targets on a team that many pundits predicted would go all the way to the Super Bowl.

The stands in Oakland-Alameda County Coliseum were packed with the Oakland Raider faithful that evening of August 13, 1978. A cool breeze was blowing in from San Francisco Bay. Not one of the 55,000 fans had an inkling of the drama about to be played out before them--nor would anyone ever forget it.

The Patriots took an early 14-7 lead and were driving again with less than two minutes remaining before halftime. A series of Grogan passes had moved the ball from the New England 13 to the Oakland 24, where it was second and 13. Coach Chuck Fairbanks sent in the call, a down and in pattern to Stingley over the middle.

That pattern had been driving the Oakland secondary--especially free safety Jack Tatum--crazy for most of the half. New rules had been developed in the off-season to give receivers more protection and produce more scoring, but this had frustrated pass defenders like Tatum who could no longer hit a receiver within five yards of the line of scrimmage. Defenders now had to time their hit to coincide with the arrival of the ball and deliver it with enough force to either jar the ball loose or leave the receiver seeing stars and listening for footsteps.

Grogan called the signals. Stingley lined up wide right, took five strides and then cut in across the middle. The ball was not thrown on time. The delay took Darryl far into the middle of the field, and when the ball finally arrived, so did Tatum, who delivered a devastating hit. Stingley ducked his head, but the top of his helmet collided with Tatum's shoulder pad. Stingley fell to the ground and lay deathly still. That one blow had changed his life forever.

"I was pretty much aware of everything that was happening," Stingley recalls. "I went up to catch a pass. I remember the hit. I was just lying on my back getting ready to get up like I did hundreds of times before.

"But I just couldn't move a thing. It felt like an elephant had his foot on my chest. I just couldn't move. I went into shock after that.

"I wanted to know that everything was going to be all right. The trainers rushed out and they said: 'just relax Darryl.' They thought it was a pinched nerve or something like that and they thought that I, being the kind of player I was, would bounce back from it. When I couldn't move, that was the indication that something serious was going on and they brought the stretcher out.

"I knew it was serious when I couldn't move, but I thought like they thought--that it was something that would resolve itself."

Team doctors fitted Stingley with a cervical collar and he was transported to nearby Eden Hospital in Castro Valley. There, X-rays confirmed the doctors' worst fear: the blow to the top of his head had driven two vertebrae together, cracking one and bruising the spinal cord. Aside from his right shoulder, there was no sensation or movement below the point of the injury.

"I had no idea what the impact on my life would be," he said. "If I could retain what I had physically, I knew I'd be all right. That was the only question I wanted answered. I asked that question from the time they took me off the field to the time I got to the hospital. When I couldn't move and when I looked down and saw them cutting my uniform off from my feet on up, I knew it was serious."

Just how serious, nobody really knew until much later. One of his lungs collapsed and he developed pneumonia. Only his excellent physical condition allowed him to pull through and stabilize himself enough for the doctors to perform a delicate operation to fuse two vertebrae together to prevent further slipping. After several months, although he remained paralyzed, he became strong enough to transfer to the Rehabilitation Institute of Chicago.

It wasn't an easy transition. "It was still a tough adjustment because you never want to give up on the possibility of regaining your movements through therapy," said Stingley. "You can't be tormented like me, 26 years of life after being the person I was, all of a sudden having to be waited on and being at the mercy of other people. To a proud person and an independent person that's difficult to deal with.

"It's basically frustrating. You want to do this for yourself, you don't want to be waited on. Just constantly, around the clock, 24 hours a day, seven days a week, 365 days a year, just constantly frustrating. You may lash out and say some things or do some things to people around you because of that frustration. It's not what you'd call a 'normal life' at all."

While Stingley's life would never again be what most would call "normal," with the help of the therapists at the Institute, he began to learn to live with it, learn his limitations, and re-group.

"I stopped asking myself why and decided that I might as well deal with it and make the best of it," he said. "That's when my life turned around. Now I know what my limitations are. If I can get somebody to help me do this, then I can do that. I became a master problem solver. If I have to go through life depending on people then I'll figure out how to communicate with people. I know if I've got to get it done, I can get it done."

It was here that Stingley's experience and training as an athlete paid dividends. "My attitude became the attitude of an athlete," he said. "I had to be a competitor. That's why I can deal with the term physically challenged. Everything I did as an athlete on the football field was a challenge. When you're going against another team, the object is to score.

"It was a challenge. A challenge I was willing to meet as an athlete. But I asked myself if I was willing to meet that as a person now. Outside of athletics, my whole life would be based on my attitude. I took the attitude from what I did all my life as an athlete, overcoming obstacles, being an overachiever, being goal oriented.

"I figured, OK, I'm left with limited movement, I can do this, but I can't do that so I'm going to make the best of it. Even without direction, I set out to make the best out of life, whatever comes my way. For a while there I still didn't know what I wanted to do with my life. Where would I fit in with this disability? I was still mentally handicapped because I was still doubtful about what my work would be."

There were other problems as well. His wife, Tina, left him, and he found that he couldn't deal with the physical rigors of a scouting and administrative position offered him by the Patriots.

"It happens to people in the disabled community," he said. "Someone loves you to death when you're healthy, but when you're challenged you become sort of a glorified older baby because you have to be taken care of, spoon fed, cleaned and changed and those things. Some people can't deal with that situation and didn't have enough love to cover that. That was one of the low points and my family situation suffered from it. I had three young sons at the time, Hank (Darryl Junior), Derek, and John (Smith).

"It got me thinking, well what do I do? So I sought the help of friends. You've heard the old cliche 'A lot of them bailed out, a lot of them stayed around?' The ones that stayed around--the ones I least expected-- they helped me get through this as well as my family. Even they had problems early on. The way my mother thought and reacted wasn't beneficial to me at the time, but all those wounds have healed.

"There isn't a handbook that is written for anybody that says 'this is what you do with a person with a spinal cord injury' or whatever. There are no guidelines, so you operate on impulse. It's based on frustration, anger and just out and out hurt. A lot of people suffered and a lot of people acted unlike I thought they would act. And some of them surprised me.

"Those were highs and lows. When you thought there was love, there wasn't any, but there was enough [from unexpected sources] to sustain and keep me going. For that whole period of time I was still the athlete, still a competitor, still determined no matter what. I will survive somehow, some way, because I have that going for me and I have God looking out for me.

"The intangibles were the people who came along that I had nothing to do with but hopefully, maybe God sent into my life. I like to look back. I never had a game plan, I never knew how this would work, I just prayed and hoped that it would, and it did. I think about it now and I'm glad all that happened because I wouldn't be where I am now. The lows make you stronger."

A little more than a year after his injury, Stingley came back to New England to watch the Patriots play in a Monday Night game on national television. At halftime, Howard Cosell asked the crowd to turn and salute him. The ensuing standing ovation lasted for nearly 15 minutes.

"That was definitely one of the high points," Stingley recalls fondly. "I keep emphasizing the energy and support you get from people, knowing that they care and that they want the best from you.

"It's not equivalent to what happens when we score touchdowns. It's ten times greater, the feeling that you get with people and their outpouring of love. Sort of like, I would say, a launching pad. Push me back out there, I say OK. People appreciate the fact that I'm still striving. I haven't given up on life and I'm going to make a go of it. When you have the drive and somebody gets behind you, there's nothing like that. They didn't forget me and they wouldn't forget me."

There have been other dreams and aspirations. Stingley received numerous awards for his courage and example to the disabled, especially youth. He lent his name to several different organizations and groups just to inspire people in some form or fashion.

"Once I got my feet back on solid ground and established communication with people. I opened up my own life to let people back in," he said. "I travelled a lot and came in contact with a lot of prominent people like Muhammad Ali, Stevie Wonder, and President Bush.

"Stevie Wonder was a major influence in my life because I naturally had known him musically, but I had never met him as a person. People magazine arranged a meeting between us in January 1980. I'll never forget it. I remember that, at that time, he wrote something down for me on an album. This was what really set me off as part of that launching pad.

"It said: 'When bad things happen to people like you and I, some people would say that it's bad, but in essence we have become a part of God's army and our purpose in life will be to make weak people become stronger people, and we shall succeed.'

"To me that put everything in perspective because it's like it happened, it's a bad thing, but what good's come out of it? I'm still alive, God left me here for what purpose?

"Just being allowed to live and just being myself would be serving God's (purpose) as well. But I decided to embrace Stevie's philosophy.

And if I can make a weaker person stronger by me just surviving and showing people I'm diligent in what I do, what happened to me was not in vain.

"I was so impressed by his being blind since birth and accomplishing what he did on the piano. That was a challenge. I couldn't even envision not being able to see. He probably couldn't envision not being able to play the piano."

One of Stingley's proudest moments came at the commencement exercises for Purdue University where, 19 years after his class graduated, he received his Bachelor of Arts degree. He took the required courses at City College in Chicago, and received a standing ovation when he was wheeled to the podium to receive his diploma.

"It was only for my own self-gratification, as well as the promises that all athletes make to their parents," he said. "I did and I'm glad that I did. I guess it was in the natural order of things because what happened as a result, was that people started saying, 'Hey, Darryl, what are you going to do now? You're back in the flow of life, what are you planning on doing with it?'

"Old newspaper articles always stressed that I loved to work with children and motivated children, especially the community I live in here in Chicago. I know that these kids can be saved if somebody takes the time to provide some positive attitudes and alternatives for them. So I decided shortly after that I would start this youth foundation. And I was looking for a catchy name and finally decided if I used my own name people might recognize it and help us."

So Stingley began to build a foundation from the ground up. He set down goals, applied for tax-exempt status, applied for grants and arranged for publicity and staffing. Today the Darryl Stingley Youth Foundation is a nonprofit corporation providing programs, activities and services that address the needs of the youth of the city of Chicago, Stingley's home town.

The Foundation sponsors mentorship, tutorial and enrichment programs, holds yearly youth days and offers a sports program and scholarships to Chicago high school athletes who exemplify the goals that Stingley set for himself through both academic and athletic excellence.

"Nobody gets paid," says Stingley of his staff. "They volunteer. They come to meetings. Everybody's contributed in some fashion, some more than others. We hope that, eventually, people can get paid. It's the proudest thing I can hang my hat on.

"I've been with kings and queens and I've been with the common man and all of them from top to bottom. I hope they all got something from me--motivation to be positive about things they want to do in life."

Stingley became a quadriplegic well before the passage of the Americans with Disabilities Act, and has seen the law's impact on the public's concept of the disabled. "I was out there before the ADA was even passed," he said. "There were lots of places where they'd have to pick up my chair and carry me in, but I was determined to get in anyway. Now places are in compliance and that's an added plus.

"I remember when United Airlines dropped my chair once. It was on my birthday. I was on my way to Boston. They dropped my chair and bent the frame. When I first contacted the airline about the damages they said it was like luggage to them, so only $750 was allowed for damages on a chair costing four or five thousand dollars."

Percy Woods, who was also confined to a wheelchair, was the president of United Airlines at the time. Stingley wrote him on behalf of himself and other physically challenged flyers. From that point on, he never had another problem. United Airlines bought him another chair.

"Anybody who has a major business or restaurant, anybody who deals with public access--and that's basically anybody you can think of-- should be in compliance with the Americans with Disabilities Act," says Stingley. "As long as they're in compliance then people like myself can go out and do things and live the best life they can from their vantage point and enjoy life like another person.

"ADA has to go further in the sense that they have to make a concentrated effort to enforce the law. I do hear from time to time 'well, we're going to be building, we're going to add a wing on and it's going to cost us this much money and if we have too many people coming in here with chairs we're going to lose money.'

"It's sensitivity that's needed also. People have to be human beings. It's not the whole thing about the handicapped or the physically challenged. It's like being a human being to your fellow man. You have an advantage, why don't you help somebody else? That's the way I see it."

Stingley points out that members of the physically challenged community are demanding more attention because of their numbers. While he is considered a pioneer for the physically challenged, he points out that there were others before him, that didn't get the national attention and the focus. He was active in Chicago in 1985 with an access living group seeking to encourage more physically challenged people to be independent.

"Marca Bristo was one of the leaders," said Stingley. "She's still on the President's Council. She was involved with the assembly and the passing of the Americans With Disabilities Act."

Stingley lives in a double condominium in Chicago that also serves as the office and headquarters of the Stingley Foundation. He uses a $14,000 computerized wheelchair which he controls with his right arm. He can sign his name with a pen fitted to the brace on his right arm and has learned to type, albeit slowly.

He continues to visit the Chicago Rehabilitation Institute to maintain his basic range of motion. He uses a telephone with a headset which he credits with saving his life. He marvels at the new innovations available for the physically challenged and the engineers and technicians who have developed them. "It's a whole new world and my hat's off to them. I appreciate them to a man or to a woman. None of them are in it for the money. They have a sincere concern about people with disabilities and how to make the quality of their life a lot better.

"That's the prevailing attitude of everybody I encounter in the rehab institute. The therapists at the rehab are more happy than you are when you can learn to write your name. When I came out, people asked me for my autograph and every time they did I thought: 'Thank God for the people in rehab and their patience with me.'

"I had one rehab person who was female, she didn't call me a sissy, but she said 'I thought you were a football player, what are you crying for?' They had me up on my arms and the pain was so unbearable. We had an understanding because I knew she was trying to help. It was just her method of trying to help that took some getting used to. I was there seven months and now I can't stand to be in anybody's hospital for more than an hour."

Several Chicago high school athletes who suffered debilitating injuries can testify that Stingley has spent considerably more than an hour at their bedsides, offering hope, encouragement, and, in some cases, financial support. Stingley remembers Kenneth Jennings, who was paralyzed during a football game.

"I actually went to the hospital a couple days after he was hurt," Stingley recalled. "They left us in a room together and I said: 'listen, you know, I know more than anybody else what you're thinking right now. I know that you're scared. I know that you're afraid, I've been where you're going.

"I know what it's like to be afraid and not know what the future may bring, but I'm here to tell you that as long as the purpose of your heart and your mind is to fight, that you're not going to give up and you do what these doctors tell you they'll get you to the point where you'll be stable enough to eventually leave this hospital.

" 'I know it's easy for me to say, but things will be OK. You'll be able to have a life. Don't think that life is over. Don't quit on yourself. Don't quit on life. There'll be things you won't be able to do, but there will be a lot of things that you will be able to do. All this is going to take time. It's not going to happen tomorrow. It may not happen next year. It may not even happen the year after that, but what you've got to do is maintain at all costs. No matter what else is going on around you, maintain a quiet determination that you're not going to give up on yourself and you're not going to give up on life." In fact, in 1983, Stingley titled his autobiography, Happy To Be Alive.

Darryl Stingley has not given up on life. In fact, he has lived it to the fullest. He has met with princes, presidents and celebrities. He runs a successful foundation. He is instrumental in reaching out to the youth of his native Chicago. In his late 40's, where does he go from here? He pauses a longtime before answering in a soft voice.

"I don't know if I have an ultimate goal unless it's to, if at all possible, stand up and take a few steps before I leave this earth. If that doesn't happen, life is full, life is good, God is great. I'm just so optimistic about the future because things look so great right now."

**Everyone Is Put Here For a Reason**

**Colleen Flanagan, National Easter Seals Representative**

### Everyone Is Put Here For a Reason
### Colleen Flanagan, National Easter Seals Representative

Colleen Flanagan was born in Worcester, Massachusetts in 1984. As many young adults do, she looks forward to her future with a mixture of positive anticipation and realistic concern. She wisely works at sorting out her potentials and her challenges. So far, she has accomplished a great deal and demonstrates wisdom beyond her years.

Currently a senior at the private Cotting School in Lexington, Massachusetts, she is able to look back at her experiences remembering some very difficult situations while reminising with a delightful sense of humor.

Colleen says that her family never told her straight-out that she had a disability. She recalls that as a small child she never understood herself to be any different than anyone else. She remembers being confronted by a five year old child asking her blunt questions and for the first time understanding that she must be different because not all children used walkers and braces or faced surgeries over and over. But she just "put it aside" and said to herself "well, this is just the way I am." It wasn't until she was about eleven years old that she began to truly realize that her lifestyle was going to be quite different because she wouldn't be able to play sports and do many of the things that other adolescents and children readily did.

When she was young, she wanted to be a baseball player. Her parents never specifically said that she couldn't play sports but when the town recreation teams were organized they often told her that one of the most important jobs in sports is being a spectator, that there wouldn't be any sports around if some people weren't spectators. In recent years as a camp counselor, she has often repeated this to young children who simply are not able to be active participants.

Colleen has Osteogenisis Imperfecta. She describes her disease as effecting her bones so they are very soft and fragile. They break a lot. Some days she can be zipping around in her manual chair or even walking on crutches and the next day experience a fracture and become completely dependent on others. "So", she says, "I have my ups and downs with my disease but it is what it is and I deal with it. I have been dealing with this my whole life and I just refuse to get depressed about it."

Colleen is blessed with a great family that she deeply loves. "I have very supportive parents," she say with a smile, "and also very supportive aunts and uncles who serve as second moms and dads and cousins who serve as second brothers and sisters. I'm very blessed in that way." She points out that if she were to decide to "pull, oh, I'm disabled and you can't make me do this or that, it just wouldn't be accepted in my house." She describes a recent Thanksgiving when the family was gathered and while they were lifting chairs and moving furniture, they were yelling at her asking whether there were enough chairs, where they should be placed, and what else should be done. She is always given a job. If she fails in hers, she is in trouble just as much as when others fail in theirs. She is proud that her family has always been supportive and loving and that they have always given her responsibilities and tasks.

Colleen has a severe form of tarda variety of osteogenesis imperfecta which results in a number of significant problems for her. Her disease makes many tasks very difficult. Difficulties began at school at the very beginning. She did not go to kindergarten because of the danger of broken bones. Children throw balls, jump around, and engage in all sorts of play activities. It was felt that her involvement would be too great a risk. She began school in the first grade at the age of five. She missed a lot of school time due to fractures and surgeries, so considering her age, it was decided that she should repeat first grade. She continued in public school for some time but inevitably missed a lot of school and the gaps in her education became more and more serious, nearly impossible to overcome. When she was about ten years old, things started to get really bad for her. She recites many examples of what she calls, "stupid little things". For example, she remembers a asphalt area of the playground, the only area she could use. There were swings and grass but she couldn't use them. There was a new gymnasium which she also could not use. She had to stay on the tar, always alone. That's when she began again to question her situation. She asked her mom if there was anyone else anywhere like her. She remembers that it was a doctor who suggested that there was a "hospital school" that she might want to see. She reacted negatively to this suggestion because of the word "hospital". However, her mom was able to explain to her that the school that was suggested was not a "hospital" at all but really a great school. They visited Cotting School where all the kids immediately talked to her. She was excited that they talked to her so willingly and naturally, not because someone said, "talk to Colleen". To use her words, "it was wild". "Wow," she said, "I love this place". She looks back to her entrance into this school as a turning point in her life. She now knows that as a result of her fine education, she has the potential to go on to college, get a good job and lead a productive life. She speaks of contributing to society, bettering herself, and enjoying new experiences. She comments on the very high percentage of people with disabilities who do not hold jobs and is grateful for the education she has received, that will allow her to move ahead with her life, to indeed some day to have a real vocation.

In school, Colleen participates in numerous activities. A gifted musician, she has been a soloist on numerous occasions. She is editor of the school newspaper and a cheerleader for the basketball team. She is so grateful that she has been free to do all these things rather than constantly using all her energy to fight off constant questions such as "why are you so short?" and the stares of others which in past years often made her so uncomfortable.

"When you are thirteen, you think everyone is looking at you", she correctly suggests. This can be true for any adolescent; it's especially true for a person like Colleen whose abilities to do many teenage activities were of necessity, limited. She is pleased that she could work on her studies so freely and appropriately so that she can now realistically look forward to college where she hopes to major in communications. She wants to work in public relations, for which her gifts are apparent.

In 1991, Colleen had the opportunity to attend Easter Seals Camp. While there she was selected as a "Queen of the Camp". She describes that experience as being selected from among several hundred campers to "wear a crown and parade around camp on a pony!" She remembers that on that day, Easter Seals Scouts were there and the next thing she knew she was talking to the Easter Seals President. She became Massachusetts Easter Seals Child and in 1994, the National Easter Seals Youth Representative. There has been only one other person from her state selected for this honor. In this capacity, Colleen represented people who she describes as"not yet adults but not children either". They were 14 to 18 years old, what she describes as "that awkward age". She represented them and talked about the issues they face including such topics as accessibility. Her activities included meeting with President Clinton in the Oval Office.

She has knowledge and understanding beyond her years. Much of this comes out of her experiences. She talks freely and clearly about conditions that effect people with disabilities. She has had many conversations with older people about realities before the Rehabilitation Act of 1971 and the recent ADA. She says, "some things are clearly better but laws are not going to fully work until general attitudes are further improved." She quickly recalls examples of negative attitudes she has encountered such as an attempt to visit a furniture store with her mom. When she asked a salesperson if there was any way she could enter the store, the salesperson could not understand what her problem was! "The stairs," she said, "I can't use the stairs." "No one ever asked me about that before," said the salesperson. "I didn't realize that was a problem." The manager upon arriving on the scene added an even stronger statement worthy of condemnation when he said, "Oh, we looked into that and it is impossible!" "How," asks Colleen, "can it be impossible to change three steps into an accessible entrance?"

Colleen much enjoyed studying about President Franklin Roosevelt. She feels that it was incredible how "he accomplished such great work even though disabled and less than 10% of the people never even knew." He is one of the people who she believes was courageous and brave and an example for others of what can be accomplished by a person so dedicated to his work.

She is grateful for the experience she was fortunate to have through Easter Seals. That experience has directed her toward public relations. She greatly enjoys talking to people and dealing with the public. She has further honed these skills in her work with the school newspaper. She has also been given the opportunity to shadow the Director of Development, Diane Newark, at her school and has participated in the planning and conducting of special events. She readily admits that there is much to learn, especially behind the scenes and she is realistic regarding how her medical problems may effect her efforts from time to time. The computer provides Colleen with opportunities that would not have existed in the past. She knows that during a period when her health might even keep her bedridden, she could still contact people and conduct business. "If I'm down for two weeks, there would be nothing wrong with my head. Everything is accessible there, everything is possible."

Colleen is a hopeful and an encouraging person. She advises other students, particularly younger ones, to learn to use the best skills they have, to realize that in many cases, they have more abilities than disabilities. With a sense of humor, she refers to politically correct language as sometimes being a nuisance. Although doesn't particularly like the word "disability", she suggests that we should not dwell on terminology. Whether it is a good word or not, "everyone has some sort of disability or lack of ability. Not everyone can sing or be an accountant or an attorney. I could say that, 'Yes, I do have a disability but I'm better than you at whatever.' You see, I just know that I can do something worthwhile. Everyone is put here for a reason. I know I have been."

# ENDNOTES

## "Go For Broke!!" Daniel K. Inouye, Senator From Hawaii

| | |
|---|---|
| 1. | Senator Daniel K. Inouye with Lawrence Elliott, *Journey to Washington*, Prentice-Hall, Inc., Englewood Cliffs, N.J., 1967, p.276. Hereafter cited as J to W. |
| 2. | J to W, p. 277. |
| 3. | J to W, p. 279. |
| 4. | J to W, p. 276. |
| 5. | J to W, p. 290. |
| 6. | Biographical material provided by Senator Daniel K. Inouye's office, p. 1. Hereafter cited as Bio. |
| 7. | Bio, p. 2. |
| 8. | J to W, pp. 152-156. |
| 9. | J to W, p. 157. |
| 10. | J to W, p. 169. |
| 11. | Interview with Senator Daniel K. Inouye, November 1995, Question 5.    Hereafter cited as Interview. |
| 12. | Interview, Question 5. |
| 13. | Interview, Question 1. |
| 14. | J to W pp. 193-5. |
| 15. | J to W, p. v. |
| 16. | J to W, p vi. |
| 17. | J to W, p. 184. |
| 18. | J to W, pp. 185-7. |
| 19. | J to W, pp. 191-2. |
| 20. | J to W, pp. 179-185. |
| 21. | J to W, p. 186. |
| 22. | J to W, p. 200. |
| 23. | J to W, p. 17. |
| 24. | J to W, p. 3. |
| 25. | J to W, p. 7. |
| 26. | J to W, p. 27. |
| 27. | Bio, p. 1. |
| 28. | J to W, pp. 40-41. |
| 29. | J to W, p. 48. |
| 30. | J to W, p. 51. |
| 31. | Bio, p. 1. |
| 32. | J to W, p. 61. |
| 33. | J to W, p. 57. |
| 34. | J to W, pp. 65-67. |
| 35. | J to W, p. 68. |
| 36. | J to W, p. 75. |
| 37. | J to W, p. 74. |
| 38. | J to W, p. 75. |
| 39. | J to W, p. 86. |
| 40. | J to W, p. 85. |
| 41. | J to W, p. 91. |
| 42. | J to W, p. 96. |
| 43. | J to W, p. 104 |
| 44. | J to W, p. 115. |
| 45. | J to W, pp. 137-38. |
| 46. | J to W, p. 123. |

47.     J to W, p. 143.
48.     J to W, p. viii.
49.     J to W, p. 201.
50.     J to W, p. 202.
51.     J to W, pp. 204-207.
52.     J to W, p. 207.
53.     J to W, p. 216.
54.     J to W, p. 209.
55.     J to W, p. 222.
56.     J to W, p. 229.
57.     J to W, pp. 231-32.
58.     J to W, p. 237.
59.     J to W, pp. 238-39.
60.     J to W, p. 241.
61.     J to W, p. 241.
62.     J to W, p. 243.
63.     J to W, pp. 248-49.
64.     J to W, p. 249.
65.     J to W, p. 251.
66.     J to W, p. 252.
67.     J to W, pp. 262-63.
68.     J to W, p. 273.
69.     J to W, p. 273.
70.     J to W, pp. 274-75.
71.     J to W, p. 288.
72.     J to W, p. 289.
73.     J to W, pp. 289-90.
74.     Interview, Question 2.
75.     Interview, Question 2.
76.     J to W, p. 22.
77.     Interview, Question 3.
78.     J to W, p. 22.
79.     J to W, p. 23.
80.     Interview, Question 3.
81.     Interview, Question 4.
82.     Interview, Question 4.
83.     Interview, Question 5.
84.     Interview, Question 7.
85.     Interview, Question 8.
86.     J to W, p. 291.
87.     J to W, pp. 291-293.
88.     J to W, p. 293.
89.     J to W, p. 293.
90.     J to W, pp. 295-296.
91.     J to W, p. 296.
92.     J to W, p. xix.
93.     Bio, p. 3.
94.     Bio, p. 4.
95.     J to W, pp. xiv-xv.